Nigerian Sculpture
Bridges to Power

Birmingham Museum of Art
April 15 - June 3, 1984

2000 Eighth Avenue North
Birmingham, Alabama 35203

Front Cover Photo: Catalogue Number 9.
Rear Cover Photo: Catalogue Number 84.

Catalogue Design: Scott Fuller

This catalogue has been funded by the Birmingham Festival of Arts Association and a grant from the National Endowment for the Arts, a federal agency.

Library of Congress Catalogue in Publication Data
ISBN O-931394-12-0

Library of Congress number 83.073603

Table of Contents

Foreword

Nigeria has produced some of the most striking and beautiful sculpture in the world. Nigerian sculpture represents a tradition which has enriched Western culture and influenced twentieth-century artists. Unfortunately, our knowledge of this field is still limited. Western culture did not "discover" African art until this century. Study of these objects can be difficult because of the perishable nature of many of them; only a small percentage of the works made in the past survive due to their composition, and to the destructive effects of the African climate. In addition, some of the objects were not made to last longer than their use in one specific ritual or celebration. Much traditional work has been destroyed or the production abandoned through European contact and rule and through changes in beliefs and practices.

Nevertheless, despite these difficulties this century has witnessed the formation of great collections and the organization of exhibitions, with the accompanying scholarship. *Nigerian Sculpture: Bridges to Power* is an exhibition which will make an important contribution to the study of black African art. Most of the objects in this exhibition date from the late nineteenth century to the present, the most recent made in 1964. This exhibition takes as its time reference the termination point of recent exhibitions emphasizing Nigerian antiquity and presents the viewer with traditional Nigerian works from the last one hundred years.

While this exhibition includes only objects of superb artistic quality, it also emphasizes the ceremonial and functional aspects of these pieces. In Western tradition a sculpture exists alone, as a work of art. In contrast, in order to fully appreciate the works of black Africa, we must understand that these objects are intended to be used, they are part of a particular setting or performance or ritual; their significance is often related to a particular dance, song or set of movements. They cannot be isolated from this context without losing some of their impact. The curator of this exhibition, Ellen Elsas, is keenly aware of this association. Her sensitive and scholarly approach ensures that we are aware of these objects in their larger cultural context.

In addition, this exhibition is important for the citizens of Birmingham and the metropolitan area. Sculptures chosen for their artistic excellence will demonstrate to a community unfamiliar with African art that these objects rival the finest examples of Western and Oriental traditions. The museum strives to represent the cultural heritage of all Birmingham citizens and this will mark the first major exhibition of African art at the museum.

We are grateful to Ellen Elsas, Adjunct Curator of African Art, for organizing the exhibition and writing the catalogue entries and introductory essay. In addition, thanks go to Robin Poynor, Guest Scholar, for his essay, to all of the lenders whose generosity made this exhibition possible, to the City of Birmingham, Museum Board and the National Endowment for the Arts for their support. Finally, we wish to extend special appreciation to the Birmingham Festival of Arts for their selection of Nigeria as the 1984 Festival Country; their selection inspired this special exhibition and their support helped make it possible.

Gail Andrews Trechsel
Acting Director

Acknowledgements

Many helped in the planning and execution of this exhibition. Thanks go to the Birmingham Festival of Arts Association and its 1984 president, Louis Willie, and 1984 chairman, Dr. Dorothy Chambers, for financial backing and enthusiastic support and to the National Endowment for the Arts. Additional funding and operating support was provided by the Alabama State Council for the Humanities. Members of the Birmingham Museum of Art staff were invaluable. Gail Trechsel, Acting Director, Richard Murray, former Director, Betty Keen, Melissa Falkner, Virginia Hillhouse, Sonya Henderson-Bailey, Marie Lichtman, Dorothy Ernst, John Bertalan, Portia Stallworth, Maude Fowler, Mary Nix, and Pauline Vines contributed time and energy to this project.

This exhibition would not have been possible without the generosity of private and institutional lenders. Birmingham lenders include Mr. and Mrs. John Bertalan, Dr. Mike Callahan, Mr. and Mrs. E. M. Friend Jr., Mr. E. M. Friend III, Mrs. Katherine Phillips Jacobs, Mr. and Mrs. Paul Kassouf, Dr. and Mrs. Clifton Latting, Kathleen Nelson and Robert Goldenberg, Dr. John Nixon, Dr. and Mrs. Robert Phillips, Retina and Vitreous Associates, Mr. J. T. Stephens, Mr. and Mrs. Louis Willie, and Ms. Odessa Woolfolk. Lenders from other cities include Mr. William Arnett, Atlanta; Charles and Kent Davis, New Orleans; Mr. Michael Gold, Los Angeles; Tony Harrison and Pat Tyson, Washington, D.C.; Leonard and Judith Kahan, Montclair, New Jersey; Hugh and Ida Kohlmeyer, New Orleans; Robert and Nancy Nooter, Washington, D.C.; Dr. and Mrs. Ralph Burton Pfeiffer Jr., Mobile, Alabama; Mr. Riccardo Salmona, New York; Paul and Ruth Tishman, New York; and Mr. Gene Willett, New Orleans. Dr. Milton Ratner, Chicago, must be singled out for his special generosity. Institutions who lent from their collections to this exhibition are the Field Museum of Natural History, Chicago; the High Museum of Art, Atlanta; the National Museum of African Art, Washington, D.C.; the New Orleans Museum of Art; the Seattle Art Museum; the UCLA Museum of Cultural History; L. Kahan Gallery, New York and Pace Gallery, New York. Thanks also go to three anonymous lenders.

Others who were generous with advice and assistance are Joanne Berens, Perry Bialor, Lisa Bradley, Herbert Cole, Stanley and Lee Elsas, William Fagaly, Scott Fuller, Joe Josephson, Flora Kaplan, Phillip Lewis, Pamela McClusky, Patricia Rector, Doran Ross, Pamela Schrestha, Janet Stanley, Richard Townsend and Maude Wahlman.

Special thanks go to Robin Poynor for his numerous contributions to this project which go far beyond his excellent essay in this catalog, Lydia Puccinelli for guidance and assistance in many ways, and Leonard Kahan for generosity with his time, his collection and his enthusiasm. Finally, my deepest gratitude goes to Bryce Holcombe, without whose initial encouragement this project would never have been attempted, and to my husband, Fred, without whose continuous support and good humor, it would never have been realized.

E. E.

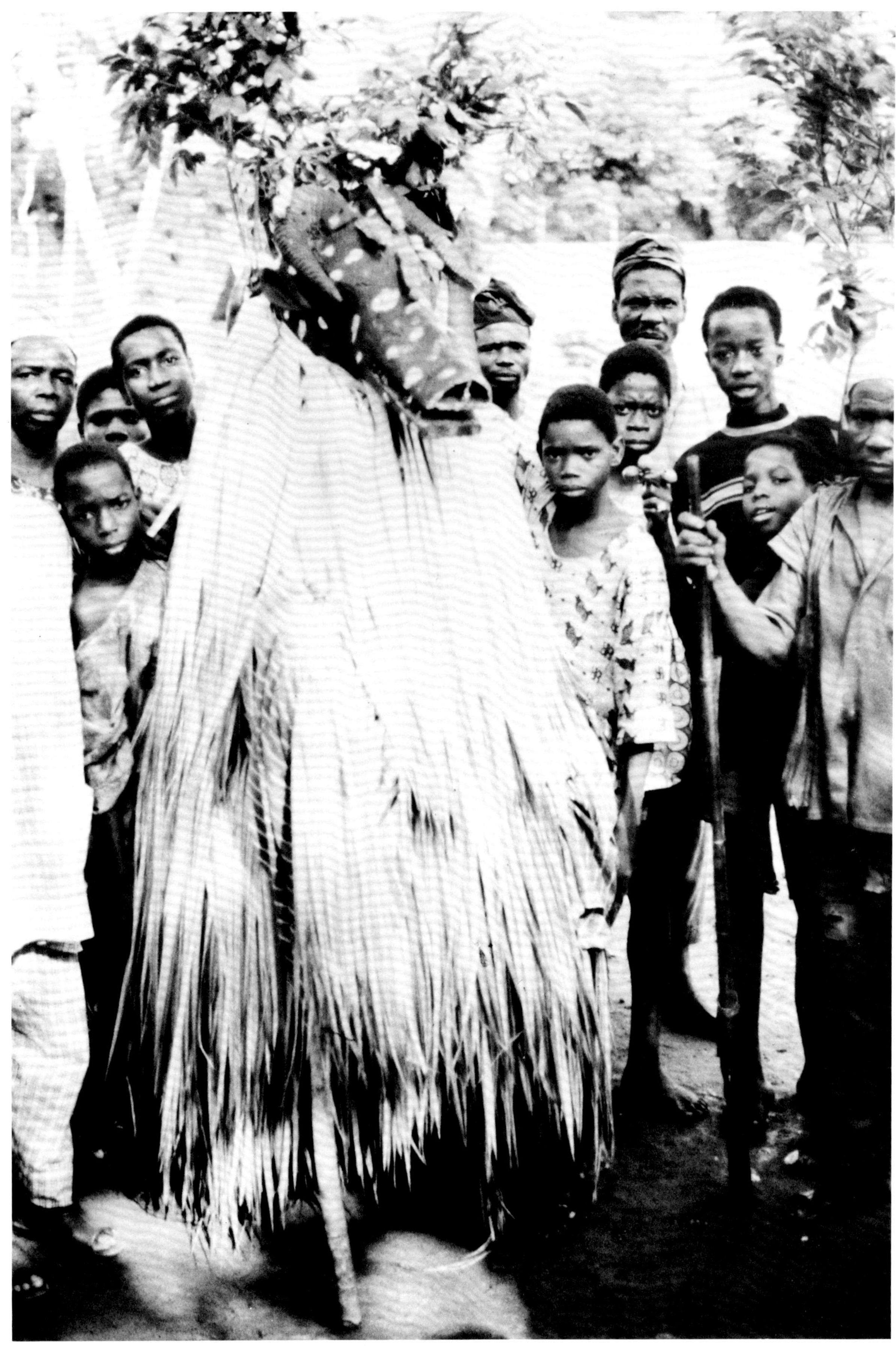

A. *Efon*, bush cow masquerade, Ipenme, Owo.

Nigerian Sculpture: Images of Power

Nigerian sculpture embodies and radiates power. Even the Western viewer, unfamiliar with the traditions from which these objects come, can sense this association from these splendid and dignified images. The power one senses is real; it derives not from the visual characteristics alone. In their original context, these sculpted objects facilitated access both to the world of the spirits and to potency, privilege and influence in this world. Power, both visual and intrinsic, can be considered the thread which unifies Nigeria's diverse sculptural traditions.

Only the more durable and portable examples of Nigerian sculpture could be included in this exhibition. In addition to wood, metal, ceramic and ivory, many other materials, not usually considered artistic media by Westerners, are used by Nigerian artists. Extraordinary objects made of unfired clay or perishable vegetable materials are found in many regions of Nigeria. The human body is used as a living canvas and may be elaborately decorated and modified; this body art may achieve high levels of aesthetic expression and philosophical significance.

Even the objects made of materials familiar through use in art of the West are seldom isolated from other means of expression. Carved wooden masks worn by dancers become part of a dynamic changing composition. Shifting visual relationships are audibly punctuated by the sounds of the anklets, beads and rattles of their wearers and the drums of the accompanying musicians. Objects other than masks are also worn, carried, handled, adorned and modified in the course of their use. Their environmental context places them within a set of rich and complex interactions which condition the way in which these works are seen. Likewise, their cultural and social context determines how they are understood intellectually and experienced emotionally.

Traditionally, these sculptures are not considered purely as art in the Western sense but as functional adjuncts to ritual activity or as delineators of social relationships. Their presence is more than decorative; it is essential. For example, Yoruba beaded crowns (cat nos. 1, 2 and 3) not only adorn a ruler and symbolize divine kingship, they transmit this institution. The crowns veil the face of the wearer, obscuring his individual identity and emphasizing the power of his office and his role as a manifestation of his ancestral forebearers. Additionally, these crowns contain powerful substances which help establish, legitimize and maintain a ruler's status.[1]

Nigerian sculpture takes many forms including crowns, masks, figures, vessels and staffs. All are alike, however, in that they partake of a physical relationship with the human body. The physical and spatial barriers between art object and viewer that are present in Western societies dissolve in Africa. No pedestal, no glass case, no frame isolate these works. Houseposts and doors define a human entry way; stools are made to be sat upon; staffs to be held. Intimacy is established when a mask is pressed against a face or when a carved figure is rubbed with palm oil, camwood or indigo. These sculptures share human space. They extend themselves within it as they are animated by their human supports and manipulators. For some objects which are charged with great spiritual powers, however, this intimacy is selective and may occur only as they are being readied for use. In performance, such objects may be surrounded by a psychological barrier. Spectators are kept at a distance as a result of their own respect or fear, or they may be prevented from approaching by the attendants of a masked figure.

These objects also possess a visual relationship with the human form. Nigerian art associated with traditional life and indigenous religions is usually representational. Its primary subject is the human face and body. Although these sculptures resemble living beings and exist in human space, they do not delude the viewer by presenting the illusion that he confronts beings identical to himself. Traditional Nigerian sculpture is rarely naturalistic; the sculptor's approach is conceptual. In art, the body is enhanced, distorted and transformed into a visible manifestation of social, spiritual and philosophical concepts. Decisions regarding form are intellectual as well as aesthetic, and formal qualities are determined by a system of beliefs and,in turn, act to shape and maintain that system. Most figures and faces are frontal and symmetrical and show a timeless ideal, not a transient moment. These sculptures are accessible in their humanness but are human representations of an extraordinary sort. They provide concrete vehicles through which one can approach abstract spiritual ideals or a desired social order.

The profound significance of sculpture is alluded to in the beliefs of the Yoruba, Nigeria's most prolific sculpture-producing people. Their mythology relates that human beings were created by the god Obatala who sculpted images from clay. The Supreme Being, Olorun, animated them with the breath of life. Babatunde Lawal, a Nigerian art historian, writes of Yoruba concepts of art and immortality: "the most important thing to note about the Yoruba notion of reincarnation is the extent to which it led them to equate the human body with sculpture, and to regard it as no more than the mask of temporal existence."[2] The Yoruba believe in the indestructability of the human soul and its potential for numerous physical manifestations.

The wearing of masks effects dramatic changes and refashioning of human appearance. Masks are an important form of sculpture in Nigeria; however, the carved wooden masks usually displayed in Western museums are only one portion of the Nigerian masquerade. They are meant to be seen as part of a total assemblage of costume, movement and sound and are often illuminated by lantern glow or firelight. The artist carves with this in mind; masks are sculpted to be perceived in a mobile context. Sometimes forms which appear overly bold or crude in a gallery setting are most effective when seen spinning and jerking in a rapid dance sequence. While some masks appear alone, others are produced to be seen as part of a large group.

Masks in Western societies serve to disguise or entertain. While serving these roles in Africa, their primary function is more profound. Modifying the appearance of the human body, they turn it into a manifestation of spiritual power. By enabling invisible forces to become visible, masks allow humans to interact with the supernatural. Their ability to mediate between these spheres make them vital adjuncts to many rituals and ceremonies.

Certain patterns of representation or visual themes can be discerned among the diverse stylistic approaches to sculpture found in Nigeria. These patterns link the works across ethnic divisions. One such pattern which appears frequently in Nigerian and other African sculpture is the emphasis on the actual body modifications and personal adornment an individual receives or wears in life.

> The body is the physical link between ourselves, our souls and the outside world. It is the medium through which we directly project ourselves in social life; our use and presentation of it say precise things about the society in which we live, the degree of our integration within that society, and the controls which that society exerts over the inner man.[3]

Enhancement of physical beauty and sexual attractiveness are important reasons for body decoration. The Tiv believe that scarification of the body draws attention to a person's best features. In addition, they scarify a woman's abdomen to increase her demand for sexual attention and to increase prospects for her fertility (cat no. 93).[4] Permanent forms of body transformation such as scarification, tattooing, tooth chipping and ear piercing can be distinguished from more temporary ones such as body painting, attire and hairdressing. The former indicate an irreversible change in status or a permanent statement of group identity. The latter indicate more transient states such as spirit possession, betrothal or mourning.[5]

Body treatment also marks a symbolic demarcation between human and animal, group member and outsider. An Ibibio puppet (cat no. 75) wears a distinctive hairdo; her face is decorated with incised marks representing scarification, patterning on her garment is carved and painted with great care. The details of her body decoration, hair and garment speak clearly of status and of civilization and its accouterments. Body decoration, transformations and adornments are intensified and emphasized in sculpture. They can be made more perfect and more permanent. Possessing the distinguishing attributes of society, sculpted forms partake of the cumulative force associated with shared identity and values. Sculpture which represents a social ideal embodies power by its correctness, its goodness and its beauty.

Analogies between beauty and moral values are seen by many southern Nigerian peoples. The Ibibio use the same term, *mfon*, to mean "beautiful" and "good" and their beautiful *mfon ekpo* masks represent deceased persons who led a moral life.[6] The elegant *mmuo* (maiden spirit) masks of the Igbo (cat no. 66) wear elaborate hairdos indicating social rank and physical desirability. They recall important ancestors and personify status, fertility, health and well-being.[7]

Anti-aesthetic or antisocial images can also express and contain power. Deliberately ugly works such as same Yoruba Egungun headdresses (cat no. 44) gain power over social deviants through their ability to satirize or criticize.[8] Beast-type masks are used in the masquerades of the Igbo, Ibibio and certain Cross River groups (cat nos. 67 and 68). These dark faces deformed by disease and violence are rough, asymmetrical and grotesque. The masks give form to negative and aggressive forces or personify ancestors of bad character.[9]

Simplifying a figure by eliminating all but the most basic and essential characteristics can broaden its reference. This approach is best seen in the carvings of the peoples living in the region of the Benue River and close to the Nigeria-Cameroon border (cat nos. 89-92). Often lacking in surface details and refinement, these elongated pole-like sculptures stand as bold, vigorous statements. Their angular forms interact with the space around them, enclosing, penetrating, dominating it. Even the smallest of these works projects a monumental quality. Simplified, abstracted images can also be found among other Nigerian ethnic groups.

Many objects, both simple and complex in form, are enriched by application or addition of other materials in the course of their use. The accumulation of cosmetic, sacrificial or medicinal deposits upon the surface and the addition of other materials add the power they contain to the object, increasing its potency. Bits of chicken feathers, blood and food offerings adhere to an *ikenga* (cat no. 60), an Igbo man's personal shrine. They form a crusty patination, a visual record of its owner's sacrifices to it over time. Each offering feeds the object and increases its potential power. Cowries, a traditional currency, hang from Yoruba dance ornaments (cat no. 26) for Eshu, divine trickster and messenger to the gods. They symbolize Eshu's association with the marketplace while adding the power of money to these already potent images. Brightly colored seeds, shiny metal and mirrors are said to enhance the visibility of certain objects. While present in these examples, additive materials have often been stripped from objects in Western collections.

In African sculpture, proportional relationships among the parts of the body are often conceived to correspond to their relative importance or symbolic significance. The enlarged heads and oversized bulging eyes of many Yoruba carvings indicate both the importance of the head as the spiritual center of the person and the spirit possession of the person by a divine force. This force "mounts. . . the inside head. . . of his priest, and the head swells. . . taking on the personality of the god."[10] The Yoruba believe that the head consists of both an outer physical aspect and an inner spiritual head which is the site of a person's essence, potential and destiny.[11] The pedestal for the thunder god Shango (cover and cat no. 9) has as its central image the face of a Shango priest. His diamond-shaped eyes protrude from his face, and a thunderstone, the symbol of the god he serves, emerges from his swollen cranium.

Figure groupings are less common than single figures. In objects in which they appear, the size of the figures may vary according to their significance. This is illustrated by a complex polychrome bowl by the great Yoruba carver Olowe of Ise-Ekiti. The bowl is held by a large kneeling figure almost four times the size of the smaller supporting figures around the base (cat no. 6).

Doubled, paired or multiple images are common in the visual representations of many African peoples. Their presence announces a multiplicity of powers. Numerous examples can be found in the objects in this exhibition. Among these are works which can be considered as "polar opposites, images which although opposite in physical, social, or metaphysical characteristics together form a unified statement of a theme."[12] The beauty and beast spirit masks of the Igbo complement one another and acknowledge the coexistence of good and bad, beauty and ugliness in this world. A portion of a prayer to the ancestors states, "The black and white cocks, the strengths and weaknesses of our society, the complementary nature of our existence are in attendance."[13] The pairing of polar opposites is also found among the Yoruba and is shown by the close association of the trickster, Eshu, the *orisha* (deity) of uncertainty, and Ifa or Orunmila, the orisha of divination and fate. Eshu's face, which announces the presence of chance into the ordered system of Ifa divination, always appears on divination trays (cat no. 29).

Repetitions of a face or image as part of a single object are another type of visual representation. The double headed Boki headdress (cat no. 84 and rear cover), the four-faced Akparabong helmet mask (cat no. 83), and the paired faces on Yoruba dance wands for Shango (cat nos. 10-14), may express "the omnidirectional powers of the being depicted."[14] Opposed heads on Cross River masks may also suggest the fundamental dualities of male/female, earth/sky, life/death and danger/beneficence.[15] Other examples of doubling or pairing include many objects made by the Yoruba: Gelede masks (cat nos. 39-41) which are danced in identical pairs, janus-headed Epa masks, Ogboni society emblems (cat no. 8) and dance ornaments for Eshu (cat no. 26). Non-Yoruba examples are also widespread (cat nos. 86, 88, 100).

Biological doubles form yet another theme represented in sculpted form. Multiple births are treated as exceptional occurrences by many traditional African peoples. The Yoruba consider twins bearers of good fortune, but the death of one or both can pose a threat to the survivor or mother. This danger can be averted by commissioning the carving of memorial figures (*ere ibeji*) to house the spirit of the deceased. Ibeji figures (cat nos. 16-22) are the best known and most numerous of African twin carvings. Protective figures for twins are also made by the Chamba (cat no. 90).

Animal representations occur in Nigerian sculpture with less frequency than those of humans. Animals are, however, depicted to symbolize human attributes or to serve as behavioral models. For example, the elephant and the leopard are associated with royal power in Benin. Formerly, the kings of Benin received one tusk from each elephant killed in their kingdom and kept tamed leopards in their possession.[16] These creatures appear frequently in the iconography of Benin castings and carvings. References to elephants appear in the sculptures of other Nigerian peoples as well (cat nos. 2, 43, 70). Symbolic and actual power derives from the use of materials from the bodies of these animals (cat nos. 30, 48, 51). Armed figures cover the carved tusk from Benin giving the tusk, the elephant's weapon,[17] many levels of associations.

The combination of animal and human attributes in a single image results in beings of intensified potency and symbolic significance. Horns, tusks and animal teeth representing masculinity and strength sprout from the heads of human figures and masks of many Nigerian peoples (cat nos. 42, 46, 57, 59, 60, 77). An Igbo title holder's ikenga shows the seated owner supporting a second figure who wears the horns of a male animal. They symbolize combativeness as well as sexual potency.[18] A human wearing an animal mask becomes an extraordinary hybrid creature. Crossing the boundaries between nature and culture, bush and civilization, he partakes of power from both realms. Horned bush cow masks used by several eastern Nigerian groups are worn for both agricultural ceremonies and funerals (cat nos. 98-100). Though aggressively animal-like in their form, subtle references to human features and body decoration confirm their composite nature.[19]

Despite distinctive stylistic differences associated with Nigeria's ethnic divisions, shared patterns of visual representation unite these objects. Recurring in the works is a consistent theme: the human face and form, transformed into splendid sculpted objects, can offer a bridge to the divine and an accessory to power in this world. These transformations separate these sculptures from the natural world; nevertheless, these works possess affecting human qualities. This combination creates a compelling tension which contributes to their visual power and to their ability to communicate across barriers of time, space and language.

Ellen F. Elsas, University of Alabama in Birmingham,
Adjunct Curator of Traditional Arts

1 Thompson, 1970. pp. 10, 74-80.
2 Lawal, 1977. p. 50-52.
3 Ebin, 1979. p. 5.
4 Bohannan, 1956. pp. 117-121.
5 Cole, 1970. pp. 12-17.
6 Messenger, 1975. p. 121.
7 Blier, 1969. p. 12.
8 Thompson, 1968. p. 65.
9 Blier, 1976. p. 9.
10 M. Drewal, 1977. p. 43.
11 Drewal and Drewal, 1983. p. 166.
12 Scheinberg, 1976. np.
13 Blier in Fraser, ed., 1974. p. 110.
14 Scheinberg, 1976. np.
15 Talbot, (*In the Shadow of the Bush*. 1912, pp. 16-17.) Cited in Blier, 1980. p. 14.
16 Ben Amos, 1980. p. 64.
17 H. Drewal, 1977. p. 35.
18 Vogel, 1974. p. 3.
19 H. Drewal, 1977. p. 51.

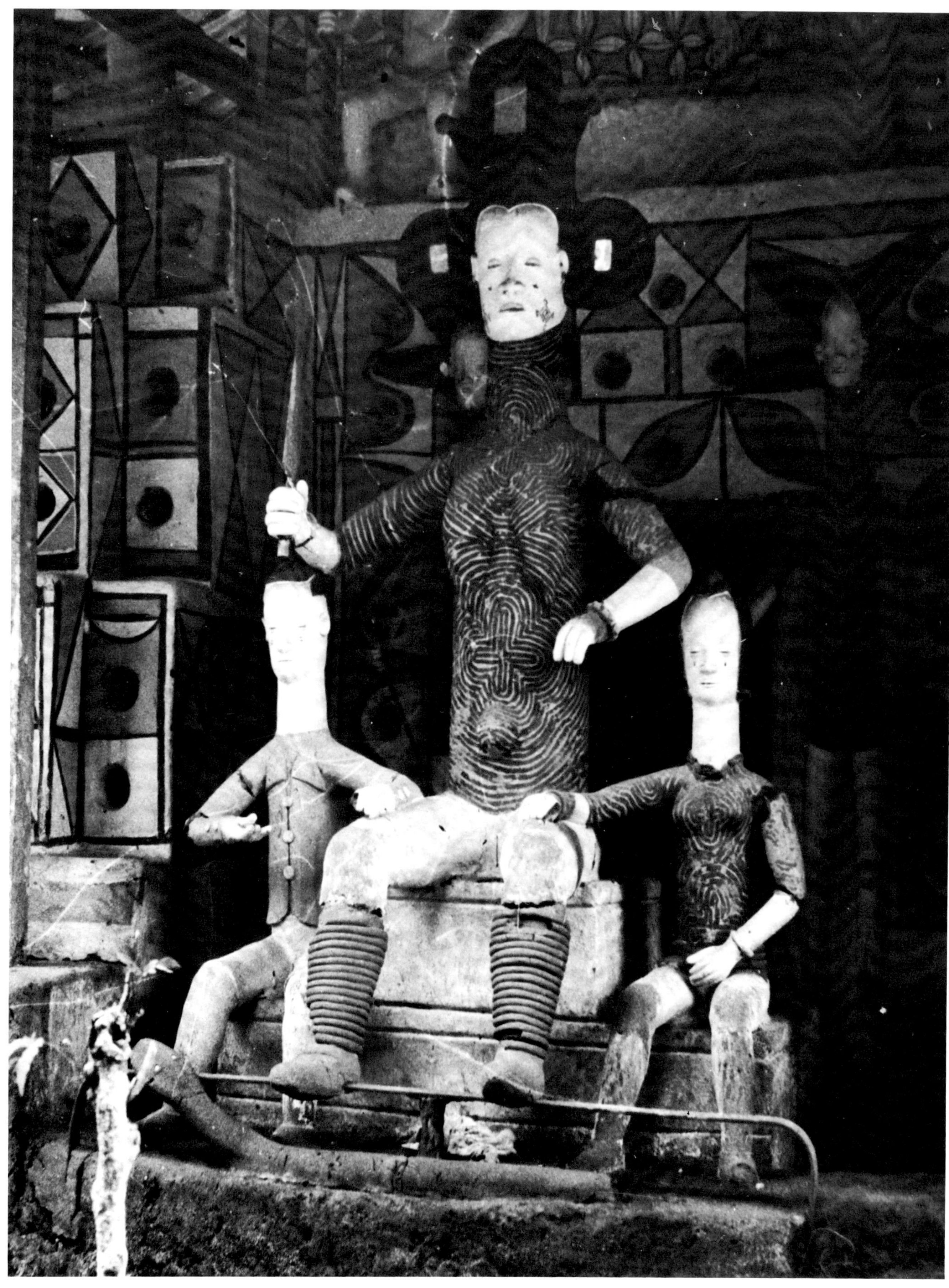

B. Mbari house, Owerri Igbo.

Nigerian Sculpture: Bridges to Power

A Worldview

In the worldview of many Nigerians, the universe is not only an arrangement of matter but also a complex system of powers. The supernatural forces and temporal powers cannot be easily isolated one from the other, for they are mutually dependent. The unseen world of spirits and the visible world of men are intimately linked as the inhabitants of either side cross bridges into the other.

Intermediaries between the two worlds abound. Divinities such as the Yoruba messenger god or the god of divination stand at the brink, leading men to the gods and the gods to men, interpreting each to the other. Ancestors bridge the void too, introducing the urgencies of their offspring to the forces that can best meet their demands and reminding their progeny of the attentions required by the gods. Kings and chiefs may be viewed as divine intermediaries, for they possess powers inherited from their predecessors, descendants of gods, to fulfill religious duties which link their kingdoms to the spiritual realm. Priests, diviners and leaders of cults stand at the boundaries of the natural and supernatural spheres, ready to provide access to those who need to cross.

Although the denizens of the supernatural realm are more powerful than those of the mortal world, their powers are in part dependent on the actions and attentions of men, for they desire the companionship and need the material offerings which the mortal world can provide. Mortals, on the other hand, depend on the prosperity and well-being that is effected by the supernatural. Thus the bridges between the two worlds are crossed incessantly as men and spirits each seek the aid of the other in the search for power.

Powers in the spiritual world are manifested in the supreme God, in deities or divinities, in spirits and in unseen forces at work in all things. Powers in the temporal world are commanded by divine kings, chiefs, heads of villages and lineages, priests and priestesses, leaders of cults, and specialists in such areas as divining, healing, smithing, hunting and warfare. Women are often believed to have special powers at their disposal. Moreover, individuals may command powers for their own use and advancement.

While sculptural forms are used as a means of communicating with the spiritual world, visual forms are rarely conceived as independent entities. They work in concert with words, music, gesture, action, dance and substance within the context of ritual. It is ritual that actually bridges the gap between the invisible world of the spirits and the visible world of men and allows the inhabitants of either to tap the powers offered by the other.

Vital Force

Although there are great differences in the beliefs and practices of the numerous ethnic groups in Nigeria, among great numbers of Africans there is the belief that the cosmos is charged with a mystical power that activates all things. This energy is at large in the universe, but it is also resident in inanimate objects as well as in animate beings. It can be harnessed by those who have appropriate training and proper knowledge. The marshalling of this energy is necessary to maintain stability and to bring increase to the community.

A useful analogy to help us understand the concept of vital force is electrical energy. It is an impersonal force. It exists in the atmosphere, but it can also be generated. It can be harnessed and localized and made to flow from one object to another. It can be channeled in specific directions. As a force, it is neither positive nor negative, but depending on the ways in which it is manipulated, it can be used effectively for good or bad. It can be stored for future use; it can be increased or decreased as needed; it can activate matter. Out of control, or in the hands of the untrained, it can maim or destroy.

Universal energy is controlled through ritual actions obtained through knowledge and training. Patrick McNaughton, in his study of the Bamana people of Mali, describes the acquisition and proper use of such knowledge in the form of recipes—"small, explicit, goal-oriented bodies of information. . . that help people carry out acts or construct certain objects."[1] These recipes may include chanting an appropriate sequence of words, combining certain animal or herbal ingredients in just the right proportions or carrying out other specified activities. Sculpture is designed to amass great stores of energy. As reservoirs of energy, sculptural forms are important supernatural devices.

Siegfried Nadel, in his study of the Nupe people of central Nigeria, recognizes the importance of ritual acts as means of harnessing a portion of the cosmic power.[2] According to the Nupe, ritual is a gift from God which serves as an intermediary, "a thing-in-between." Ritual acts are not mere acts, but forces themselves, each with a power of its own for controlling a portion of the universal energy, channeling it into effectiveness.

God

Although vital energy is at large in the universe and resident in matter, most Africans believe in the existence of a supreme Being who created the universe and set energy and matter in motion. In most instances, the High God is distant and is seldom approached directly. He has no shrines, no priests, no direct sacrifices or worship. Art forms are rarely made for the High God.

In a general sense, it may be stated that representations are not needed for a god who is not in direct communication with people. C. N. Ubah's study of the religions of two Igbo subgroups indicates such:

> Symbolic representations are important when people have a compelling need to ask the favour of, or to appease, the relevant object of worship. But the Supreme Being does not concern himself with their affairs. . . .[3]

The High God, who is the creator and source of energy, chooses to channel power to mankind through lesser spirit beings. It is through them that humanity most often partakes of the divine energy, and it is for them that great amounts of artistic energy are expended in creating objects.

Spirit Beings

While vital energy is at large in the universe as an impersonal force activated by God, it is also particularized in very personalized supernatural beings. Humans may tap these sources for the generating, renewing or increasing of their own vital energy, and in the ritual act increase the power of the divinity as well. For example, the Yoruba believe that blood contains *ashe*, power and authority. The letting of blood in ritual sacrifice

> . . . releases a vital force that is transferred to the god or spirit to renew his or her *ase* [ashe] for the purpose of benefitting the devotees. . . . The act of sacrifice is a reciprocal affair between man and the gods in which the devotee nurtures the spirit of the divinity in exchange for increased protection and blessing.[4]

Certain higher spirit beings may be called gods or divinities.

They generally have distinct personalities and attributes and will have organized fellowships of devotees led by priests and priestesses. These public cults conduct regular cycles of ceremonies in which the deity may be fed, clothed, offered gifts and communed with.

The personalities of deities often reflect their functions and the way they fit into the philosophical constructs of the people to whom they are important. To cite an example, the principles of certainty and uncertainty are basic philosophical concepts among the Yoruba. They are personified in the Yoruba gods (*orisha*) Eshu and Orunmila. Eshu is the embodiment of uncertainty, chance, violence, disorder; Orunmila of certainty, fate, destiny, balance, order. Yet the two are inseparable friends and cohorts. To approach Orunmila, one must first deal with Eshu. Both are conceived as mediators between the world of the supernatural and the world of men.

Eshu tricks men into offending the gods. Then men must sacrifice and it is Eshu who takes sacrifices from men to the gods. Thus, he is the mediator, through whom all mankind must make amends with the orisha. Orunmila is the mediator through whom mankind can discover which sacrifices must be made and what rituals must be performed to gain blessings. The two work hand-in-hand to bridge the uncertain gap between humans and the spirits.

Other spirit forces may not have such precisely defined personalities nor have large followings over broad geographical ranges, yet they may be perceived as having very precise functions with the context of the human community. Among some groups of Northern Igbo, for example, there are deities who are personifications of the four days of the week. According to Cole, these usually become the most important tutelary deities of their towns. Their cults honor them out of the fear of the potential wrath they may loose upon human transgressors.[5]

Special relationships may develop between a spirit and an individual or a family who begins to regard it as a personal tutelary spirit. This sort of spirit may be entirely capricious and may make the individual human walk a very narrow path. Mammy Wata is such a spirit. She is found all along the coastal area of Southern Nigeria among the Yoruba, the Igbo, the Ibibio and the Ogoni and appears to individuals as a mysterious and beautiful woman who lures men into her control. She lavishes them with gifts of money and riches, but she is a very jealous spirit lover. She may strike out at any who cross her. She can drive her devotees into insanity.

Most tutelary spirits come from the world of nature as opposed to the world of men.[6] The bush is a special place. It encompasses a powerful and uncivilized sphere where many powers are at work. Those who penetrate it regularly, such as hunters and herbalists, must have the knowledge of working with the powers which exist there.

Witches

The deep-seated belief in witchcraft is ubiquitous in Nigeria. Some human beings are believed to have supernatural powers which they can use against their fellow humans for their own selfish gain. The power is usually associated with women. Raymond Prince, in his psychiatric studies among the Yoruba, was told that witches are the rulers of the world and receive their power from God. They have no mercy and can kill at whim.[7] They can control human reproduction. They interfere with childbirth and can kill small children. Yet, witches are not totally evil. They protect those they choose to protect. They bring wealth to their favorites.

There are a number of ways that the human community can deal with witchcraft, for it is not a rampant and uncontrolled power. According to Yoruba myths, when women went to Eshu and asked for their special powers, he sent them to Orunmila and Olorun, the Yoruba High God. Orunmila would not allow them power until they promised to respond to certain signs as protective agents for human beings. The red parrot feather is such a sign. It may signify a witch or the powers used to control witchcraft.

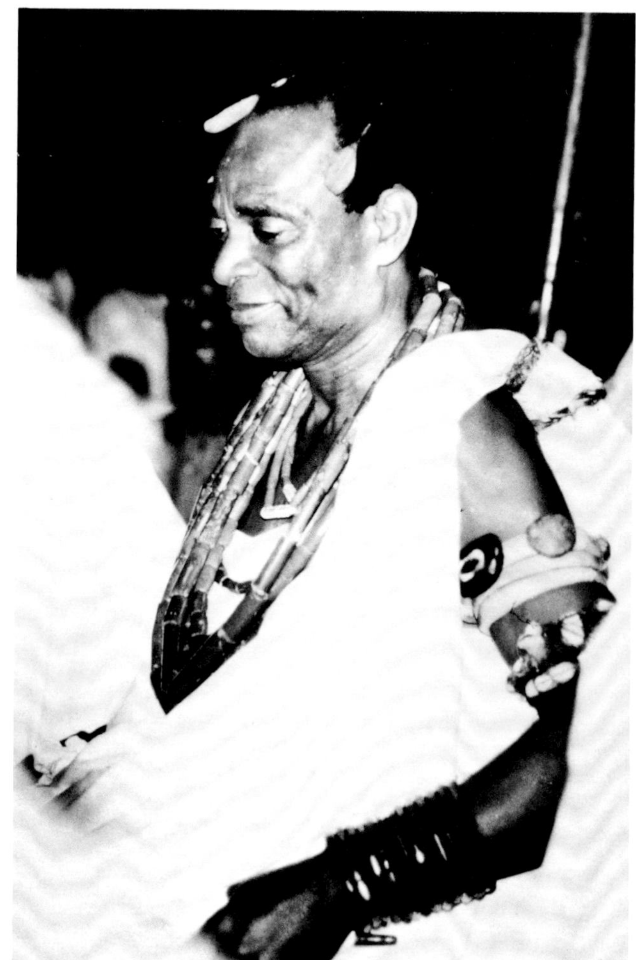

C. The Olowo of Owo at the annual Igogo festival.

Certain divinities specialize in protecting against the negative powers of witchcraft. Osanyin, the orisha of herbalists, is especially effective. His priests once fought witches with equal power. More recently the powers of witches are seen as so powerful that priests have joined forces with them, offering them sacrifices to appease them on behalf of their clients.[8]

Certain institutionalized roles contend with the powers of the witches. Yoruba *obas* (rulers) perform rituals in which evil powers are driven from the community. In Owo, the Olowo (ruler) protects his own person with amulets and charms (see photograph C) as he dances in purification rituals for his subjects. Red parrot feathers, the sign of witchcraft, hang over his forehead. Among the Yoruba several cults work against them. The *Oro* men's society exercises an extreme amount of power as the agency for carrying out the edicts of the awesome Ogboni cult. Oro's power is so great that markets close when they make a ritual appearance; all women and children and non-members lock themselves indoors. The mysterious cult has the power to cleanse a town of the evil powers associated with women—witchcraft.[9]

Egungun is a cult often associated with the spirits of the dead. Its members share in the spiritual powers of the ancestors. In the Owo area, one of the main functions of the Egungun society is to protect against witchcraft. In the past, they organized witch hunts and punished witches. Their powers are used to purify the town of evil. During the ceremonies of the *efon egungun*, the diviner and hunters who accompany the masquerader chant:

If there are witches,
Clear the way of *efon*.
Clear the way.
The *ifa* oracle supports us today.
We will be safe from the eyes of evildoers today.
All witches, clear the way.[10]

Among the southwestern Yoruba, a quite different approach is taken. Rather than fighting the witches with an equal or greater contrasting power, the *Gelede* cult chooses to placate the witches, called "our mothers," to entice them to side with the community.

The Gelede society produces spectacles which honor and serve spiritually powerful women (see photograph I). The belief that the hidden power of women is necessary for existence, according to the research of Margaret and Henry Drewal, suggests that the power of the mothers is great or greater than that of the orishas.[11]

Ancestors and the Dead

Most Africans believe firmly in life after death. It is often believed that when a person dies, his spirit remains near the place where he lived. Rituals may be performed to convince it to seek the company of his predecessors in the spiritual realm. The spirit may or may not be reincarnated, depending on the circumstances of death and burial and the quality of life lived.

The Igbo call the souls of the good, *mmuo.* They live in the world of the spirits and serve as intermediaries who relay the prayers of their living kin to the High God. They are honored and are invoked daily.[12] Witches, evil sorts, useless misfits, those who died unnatural or violent deaths and many others become bad spirits. They are a terror for the living, responsible for vicious and terrible acts.[13]

The spirits of some humans may attain the special rank of ancestor. Ancestors are a specific class of the dead. Not all dead enter this class. To become ancestors, the dead must both have proved themselves of value in the social structure while they were living and have living descendants who can perform proper rituals. Once the proper rituals have been made to install them as ancestors, they are believed to have special mystical powers which they can exercise on behalf of their living family. Their care and benevolence can be assured through proper attention to their needs. Neglect may bring about their ire and punishment.[14]

Sculpture as Bridge to Spirit Power

Great numbers of art objects are created to be used in communicating with spirit beings and in the tapping of spirit force. In the following paragraphs some of these objects and their functions in spirit manipulation will be discussed.

Representations of Spirit Beings

Some dieties or spirits are directly represented in sculptural form. The figure becomes a focal point in communicating with the spirit. For example, a number of Northern Igbo towns have cults honoring gods associated with the four days of the Igbo week. The cults and their gods are symbolized by carved figures (see cat nos. 61-64). Each god is provided with an actual compound consisting of several buildings on a sacred plot. He lives there with an entourage of immediate family—also represented by sculpted forms. Every fourth day the figure is taken out, dressed and given offerings. Once a year, he and his immediate family, along with carved representations of his extended family are congregated for a feast and purification ritual, to receive the offerings and prayers of the townspeople.[15]

In this instance, the anthropomorphic representation of the deity is a physical entity. It is visible and can thus be the focal point in the directing of prayers and messages. The devotees are entirely aware that such objects are mere representations which will decay. Yet the spirit force uses it as a point of contact for his followers.

Sculpture can be more than a mere representation. The Ijo people refer to figures as the "forehead of the spirit."[16] A person's forehead is associated with "that which rules his fortune." Thus the sculpture controls the destiny of the spirit for whom it is made, and, hence, he who controls the sculpture controls the spirit. The Ijo also refer to sculpture as the "name" of the spirit. The equating of the name of something and the thing itself is common in Africa. Horton documents a Kalabari proverb which states that "spirits stay and come in their names."[17] Whatever is done to the name is done to the bearer of the name; what is done to the sculpture is done to the spirit. By associating spirits with sculpted forms, humans can settle them in a specific location where they can be controlled.

The Ijo also call masks "names" of spirits. The carved wooden portion of the mask (see cat no. 57) is sometimes not even visible to the human audience. Its function is not to impress spectators, but to gain the presence of the spirit through possession. Horton emphasizes that the Kalabari Ijo mask is "first and always an instrument for localizing the spirit it represents."[18]

The Urhobo, neighbors of the Ijo, also use masks to depict and gain the presence of spirit forces—the *edjo* (see cat no. 56). Perkins Foss records that numerous masquerades appear in festivals, the most effective means for attracting spirits. The presences within the masks are lured to the land by a woman who dances from the creek to the land carrying a calabash of medicinal water which she sprays into the air, creating a watery bridge for the edjo.[19]

Gifts for Spirit Beings

Sculpted forms may not represent or localize the spirit at all. Some objects may be offered as something to please the spirit. The Owerri Igbo have evolved an artistic form which is one of the best examples of art as a gift. They believe that although the near gods, *agbara*, are providers, protectors and bringers of blessings, they react violently when neglected or offended.

When crises occur, the Owerri Igbo read them as signs of unhappiness from one of the agbara. When a number of problematic events take place, the elders seek the advice of a diviner. Readings may indicate that the signs were sent by an angry spirit, offended by the community. The offering that must be made as a placation is called *mbari,* a series of rituals and events taking place over several years and involving the participation of an entire community of "spirit workers." These workers are secluded within an enclosure to build an intricately designed set of buildings on whose verandahs are grouped elaborately modeled figures of clay (see photograph B). These represent the major deity to whom the complex is dedicated, other agbara, mythological characters and humans interacting in daily activities. Herbert Cole, who studied the phenomenon, refers to mbari as "an edifice of symbols."[20] Mbari is done not because people want to make it, but because the angry god has demanded it. In the act of creating a complex of beautiful forms, the community responds to the punitive powers of the deity but acknowledges its beneficient powers as well. There are no mystical powers associated with the objects themselves. They are a sacrifice to the god as was the service, isolation and activity of the workers. After the gift is presented, it is left, unmaintained, until it is overtaken by bush and crumbles away.[21]

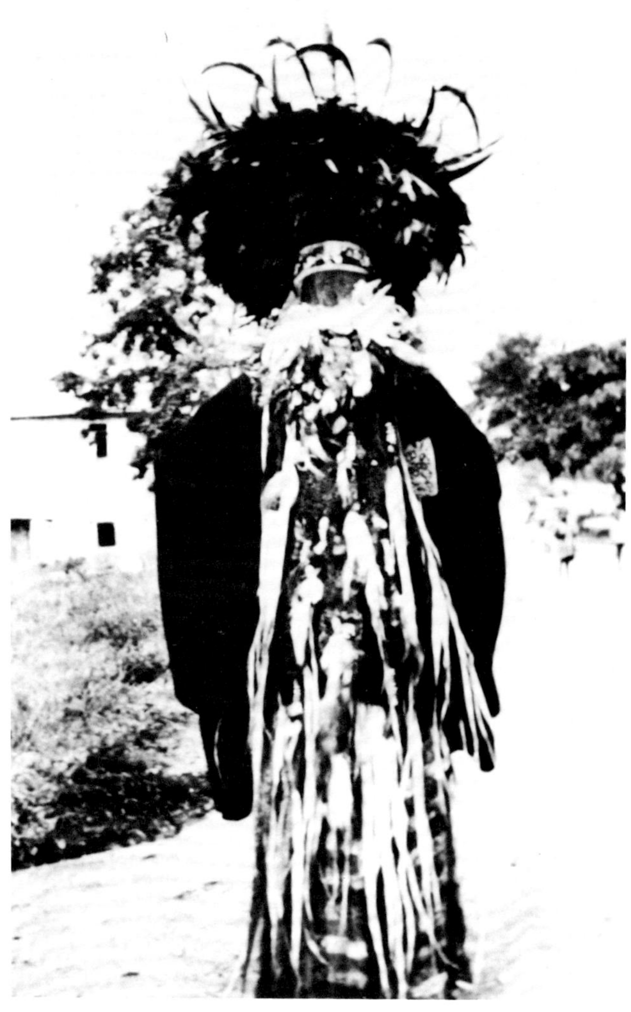

D. *Egun Aladoko,* Owo.

Sculpture as Symbolic Reference

As a rule, the Yoruba do not create images to represent the deity, the exception being for Eshu, the trickster god, who is symbolically presented in sculptural forms used in his worship. His roles are numerous and his personality complex. The iconography associated with him is just as confusing, yet Eshu symbolism is instantly recognizable. The various symbolic elements directly relate to the enigmatic personality of the prankster deity.

His most important symbol is his long-tailed hairdo (see cat no. 24). Eshu's priests wear their hair in a similar manner. Margaret Drewal interprets the hair style in the light of a phenomenon known as *osu.* Osu is a mixture of elements constituting the ashe (vital force) of the gods which is applied to incisions on the scalp of the priest and rubbed in to be absorbed into the system. A tuft of hair grows over this area, while the rest of the scalp is shaved. The priest becomes an intermediary for the god.[22] Like his priest, Eshu plays the role of intermediary, stationed between the realms of man and gods.

Joan Wescott, in her pioneering study of the iconography of Eshu, interpreted other symbolic elements in his sculpture. The black paint which covers most images refers to his wickedness. The contrast between black and the white of attached shells pertains to his activity in extremes. Miniature calabashes (see cat nos. 24 and 25) make reference to medicines, implying the magical powers Eshu controls. The whistle he often holds to his mouth (see cat no. 23) suggests his role as herald. It, along with the pipe he smokes, alludes to disregard for authority, for whistling and smoking are taboo in the palace. Cowrie shells and coins which cascade from Eshu figures (see cat no. 26) are statements of Eshu's involvement in economic affairs. Combs, mirrors, spoons, knives and clubs suspended from the figure reiterate his vanity, refer to sacrifices made because of his demanding nature and underscore his aggressive and destructive powers.[23]

Eshu may be seen on palace doors, lintels or veranda posts or in the art forms associated with numerous other gods. Small images of Eshu appear in their shrines, for he interacts with each and serves as intermediary between them and men, acting as the carrier of sacrifices between them.

Eshu's companion, Orunmila, is also an intermediary. His system of Ifa divination is the means through which a Yoruba discovers his destiny and how to deal with the forces which influence his life. Objects of high aesthetic merit are especially prolific for Ifa (see cat nos. 29-36), and while Eshu is depicted on a number of them (see cat no. 29), Orunmila himself is never depicted. Trays, cups, bowls and tappers used in the Ifa process are almost always finely carved and worked with pleasing and harmonious designs. In spite of the variety of forms, each object conveys a sense of order, balance and harmony, characteristics of Orunmila himself.

Each object comprising Ifa paraphernalia plays an important bridging role. The cups which store the sacred palm nuts are called "the dwelling place of Orunmila."[24] Palm nuts are the instruments of divination left behind by Orunmila so that men have access to the knowledge of their destinies. A miniature ivory carving of Eshu's head may be placed with the palm nuts in storage and next to the tray in the divination process, reminding the diviner and the supplicant that Eshu is there to bear messages. An ivory tapper invokes the presence and attention of Orunmila. The tray depicts the face of Eshu, so that he overlooks the ritual and lends his ashe to the utterances of the oracle. It is on the surface of the tray that sacred verses make themselves known through orderly configurations of marks determined by the casting of the sixteen palm nuts.

Karin Barber[25] suggests that an orisha's power depends on his devotees. Without followers, the god fades into insignificance. Part of the god's splendor is his earthly shrine—furnished with symbolic references to his power, gifts that mark the attention paid by his followers.

These objects, like the mbari of the Igbo, are beautiful forms to be admired by the orisha and the worshipper alike. But they also serve as symbolic devices. There are iconographical elements, symbols, color combinations and materials that have become associated with specific deities.

Shango, the powerful god of thunder, is the recipient of a large number of artistically created objects (see cat nos. 9-15). His worshippers carry beautiful staffs topped by a double axe motif. The axe represents stone celts "discovered" at sites where lightning has struck. These thunderstones represent the awesome power of Shango, symbolic of the active role he plays in the lives of his followers. Carved celts springing from the head of a figure signify the presence of the deity through possession.

Not all Yoruba divinities will have instantly recognizable symbolic elements on their sculptural gifts. These sculptures may be referred to as generic, and when they are removed from the shrine, their forms do not necessarily give clues as to which of the numberless deities they honored. As a matter of fact, they may be misleading. Ogun, the fierce god of iron, patron of warriors and all who work with metals, is a capricious and violent god. Such "hot" gods are usually associated with the color red. The figure in this exhibition represents one of his followers (see cat no. 27) carrying a sword. The coating of white on the figure is out of character for such a "hot" god as Ogun. White is associated with the calm, composed "white orishas." Pemberton records that figures associated with Ogun are occasionally found on the altars to white orishas, where all sculptures, even those for Ogun, are painted white.[26]

Sculpture for Tutelary Spirits and Bush Spirits

Some spirits develop special relationships with individuals or with groups. These alliances occur because of the mutual benefits each side can gain. Leon Siroto points out that spirits want material things. They even long for tangible bodies.

> This materialism on the part of invented spirits draws them into association with humans and provides entry into the world that humans perceive. . . . Invented spirits can crave the good things of life: physical beauty, personal adornment, companionship, solicitude, food, drink and music. They expect to gain these favors in return for the powers that they can exert on behalf of their human benefactors, both living and dead.[27]

These spirits may be represented by figures or by masquerades which incorporate human features or hybrid human and animal features.

Tangible bodies may be taken by spirits through possession or masquerades. Among the Etsako peoples, all masked performers are referred to as spirit-figures. These may represent spirits of the dead or nature spirits. According to Jean Borgatti, a number of forest spirits appear in the *Okakagbe* masquerade as anthropomorphic characters dressed in beautiful cloth appliqué costumes (see cat no. 55). The display of the elaborately and complexly costumed spirit beings appears for entertainment during festivals of worship. The senior character in the festival is Ancient Mother, an old woman with long, flat breasts, one who has nursed many children. She is accompanied by about five other masqueraders in human form.[28]

In contrast to the anthropomorphic characters which accompany Ancient Mother, one masquerade represents a bush monster. Borgatti describes it thus:

> The bush beast, Idu, rears a magnificent and horrific head featuring the broad horns of the buffalo or bush cow and a variety of antelope horns. The face, anthropomorphic but snaggletoothed, is modelled in gum, beeswax, or clay. A row of peccary tusks protrudes from the mouth. The body covering consists of overlapping split seedpods sewn onto a net costume or dried, bush raffia.[29]

The combination of human and animal forms is not uncommon in Africa. Many masquerades combine the characteristics of a variety of animals—including bush cow, crocodile, hyena, antelope and wart hog. To these may be added references to birds, snakes, chameleons, scorpions and other small wild animals. The costumes are often made of raffia, leaves or grasses to which seeds, shells, animal skulls or fur may be attached. The effect is to create a hybrid that proclaims the powers of the bush temporarily controlled for the use of humans.

Many Nigerian masks suggest the power of the bush through the depiction of the bush cow or buffalo. In Owo, the *egungun efon* (see photograph A) represents the buffalo. The purifying role of this masquerade is suggested by the tiny birds, carved separately, which fly around its head. Among the Yoruba, birds are symbols of witchcraft. As the efon masquerade leaves its sacred grove to come in to the town, its followers chant songs that warn evil forces to leave.

A number of similar horizontal masks incorporating bush cow imagery in association with other animal forms are used by several groups along the Benue River. These masqueraders often behave wildly, having to be restrained by the men who accompany them. They act as the dangerous beings they represent, yet they can be controlled temporarily (see cat nos. 98-100).

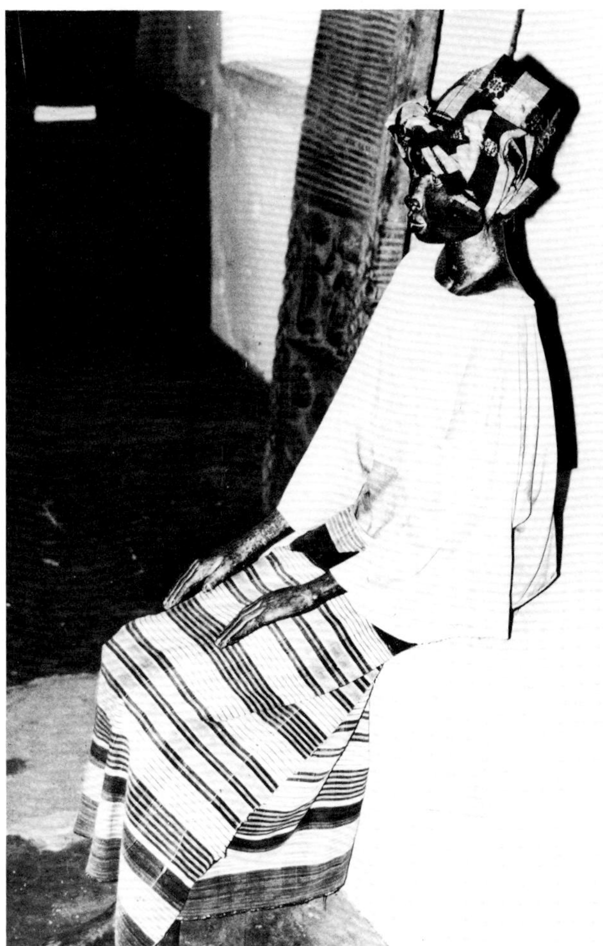

E. *Ako*, second-burial image, Owo.

Sculpture and the Witches

The mysterious and dreaded powers of the witches inspire many art forms which are meant to control or curtail activities which interfere with human productivity and happiness. In spite of their terrible potency, witches are limited in how they may use their powers, for certain signs and symbols have been given to human beings for protection against them.

The most common symbol for a witch in Nigeria is the bird or feather. Witches can leave their bodies at night and fly about as birds, doing evil, meeting in tree tops with other witches, attacking victims. Both the Bini and the Yoruba use forged iron staffs surmounted by representations of birds in combatting the evil witches. The Yoruba version of this staff often shows a large, single bird hovering over a circle of sixteen lesser birds.

Other specialists who have been given power to counteract the evil powers which prey upon the community may use bird imagery as well. Kings of Yorubaland wear red parrot feathers or white feathers of the egret on their persons during purification rituals for their kingdoms (see photograph C). Small, bead-covered representations of birds are attached to the sides of the crowns of Yoruba rulers, and a bird often sits on its peak (see cat nos. 1, 2 and 3). Again, the bird-over-bird configuration calls to mind the ritual specialist whose powers are superior to those of the malignant witches.[30] Thompson submits that

> . . . the gathering of the witches in the night at the top of the [tree], the positioning of the iron birds at the top of the medicine staff, and the gathering of birds at the summit of the headgear of the ruler suggest parallel

idealist metaphors of the transformation of doom into human survival.[31]

Other institutions which fight witchcraft may also use bird imagery in their battles with the dark powers. The efon masquerade headdress (see photograph A) has already been discussed above. The small birds which swarm around the head of the beast warn witches of the powers which the masquerade has to rid the community of negative powers. Another Owo egungun, *Aladoko* (see photograph D), makes use of hundreds of feathers in its headdress and in the raffia costume. The myriad of feathers symbolically represents "all the birds of the world," a reminder to the witches that their powers are matched by those of the cult.

Art is thus used to control the evil forces of witchcraft through actively fighting it and trying to neutralize it. Not all efforts to control the powers of the mothers are negative in impact. As Robert Thompson cautions

> The witch, after all, is an elderly person, susceptible to the pleasures of honor and entourage. As the rulers may be praised and at the same time be reminded of their obligation to the people, so the witch may, upon being honored and recognized, become responsible. Respect assures continuity.[32]

So it is that in the southwestern portion of Yorubaland the efforts to control witchcraft will be through humoring, placating and appeasing the mothers. The Gelede society provides fantastic spectacles in which song, music, poetry, dance and beautiful visual forms honor them and encourage them to use their powers for the good of the community (see cat nos. 38-41 photograph I). Henry and Margaret Drewal suggest the elaborate spectacles performed for the mothers can be seen as a "... sacrifice designed to placate ...."

Performances in which masks appear are meant to praise and honor the powers of the witches. The night time *Efe* masquerade implores powers greater than he to intervene on behalf of the community. He attempts to please these beings by teaching traditional attitudes and by ridiculing all who go against their wishes. Themes represented in the afternoon Gelede performance include all types of individuals from within and without Yoruba society as well as concepts relating to the forces of the cosmos.[33] The Drewals interpret the intent of the Gelede masquerade and dance to be to

> evaluate the state of the world through visual praise, humor, or ridicule .... the resulting ensemble, the layers of meaning, are conceived not merely for dramatic effect but for spiritual efficacy. In the presence of the mothers, the element of the masquerade ensemble, separately and collectively endowed with force, compels the maintenance of human values.[34]

Art for Spirits of the Dead

Death and the belief in the continuation of existence in afterlife have been major inspirations for creating art in Nigeria. Art used in funerals or elaborate ceremonies that take place after death help the living to reorder the social structure after the demise of a family member. The older and the more influential a person was, the more elaborate the rituals. The funeral of an elder is a time of rejoicing, of celebrating achievements and of honoring his memory, but it is also an event which separates the spirit of the deceased from the ranks of the living and installs it properly among the spirits of the dead.

Funerals may be quite elaborate and expensive. Certain high-ranking chiefs in Owo may be honored after their actual burials with what is referred to as *ako* (second burial). A life-sized articulated figure (see photograph E) is commissioned to be carved during the ritual period. When finished, it is dressed and placed in a specially decorated alcove of the home, where women sing praise songs in honor of the deceased. On the final day of the celebration, the figure is paraded through the town, accompanied by throngs of family, friends and well-wishers. At ritual points along the way, the figure is set down and sacrifices are made in its honor. It is finally buried in the grave of the deceased.

Funeral celebrations are often marked by the appearance of masquerades. The masquerade may actually impersonate the dead, advising the living how his property is to be divided and presenting in spirit form a last will and testament. In other instances, masked dancers may merely provide entertainment in honor of the deceased as is the case of the *Mangam* cult of the Mama. Mangam employs bush cow masks to entertain at funerals (see cat no. 99). Similar masks are used by the Goemai and Jukun in cults whose names are obviously related etymologically to that of the Mama.

Sculpture for the Returned Dead

Not all spirits of the dead are settled well in the realm of the spirits. Many groups believe that certain categories of the deceased are doomed to wander aimlessly. Masks which depict these unfortunate beings are clearly grotesque in the eyes of their makers. They represent ugly, darkened skulls, deformed humans with protruding and twisted features, diseased humans with all sorts of sores, lumps, bumps and eaten-away features and dangerous composites of animal monsters with threatening features such as fangs, horns and beaks (see cat nos. 67, 68).[35] They suggest a threat to society made by the souls of these evil persons. They act to keep these spirits in their proper places.

On the other hand, masks that represent the ghosts of those who lived a good life and who maintain friendly relationships with the living, serving as intermediaries with the gods, are represented in aesthetically pleasing forms. They are naturalistic and lightcolored, decorated with beautiful materials such as mirrors, ribbons, combs, dolls and other bright objects. Their costumes are brightly colored and richly decorated (see cat nos. 55, 66 and 87).

Sculpture for the Ancestors

Special human spirits that are ultimately important to the living are the ancestors—specific, named forebears who are approached for specific types of help. The ancestor, with access to the supernatural world and his understanding of the mortal world, is an ideal link between the two. Most Africans revere the ancestor and look to him for guidance as well as for intervention in daily affairs.

Although there are not as many representations of ancestors in art as was once suggested, there are numerous art forms that are used in rituals venerating ancestors. A few of these are representations. The Owo ako figure discussed above is in some ways an ancestor figure, since it is meant to install a specific named deceased ancestor into the ranks of the spirits.

Among the Oron Ibibio, elaborately carved wooden figures are made to represent a particular male ancestor (see cat no. 76). K. C. Murray stated that the carving was a place where the spirit of the dead could be conveniently approached. Although the figure itself was not worshipped, it became a thing of great holiness because it was a symbol of the deceased.[36]

Among the Mambila, shrines erected for the ancestors house a number of figures (see cat nos. 95, 96 and 97). These may represent the ancestors themselves, serving as temporary dwelling places for their visits to the shrine. Some, however, are guardian figures which protect the shrine from evil influences.

As emphasized in much recent literature,[37] not all carvings used in the context of ancestor veneration are representations

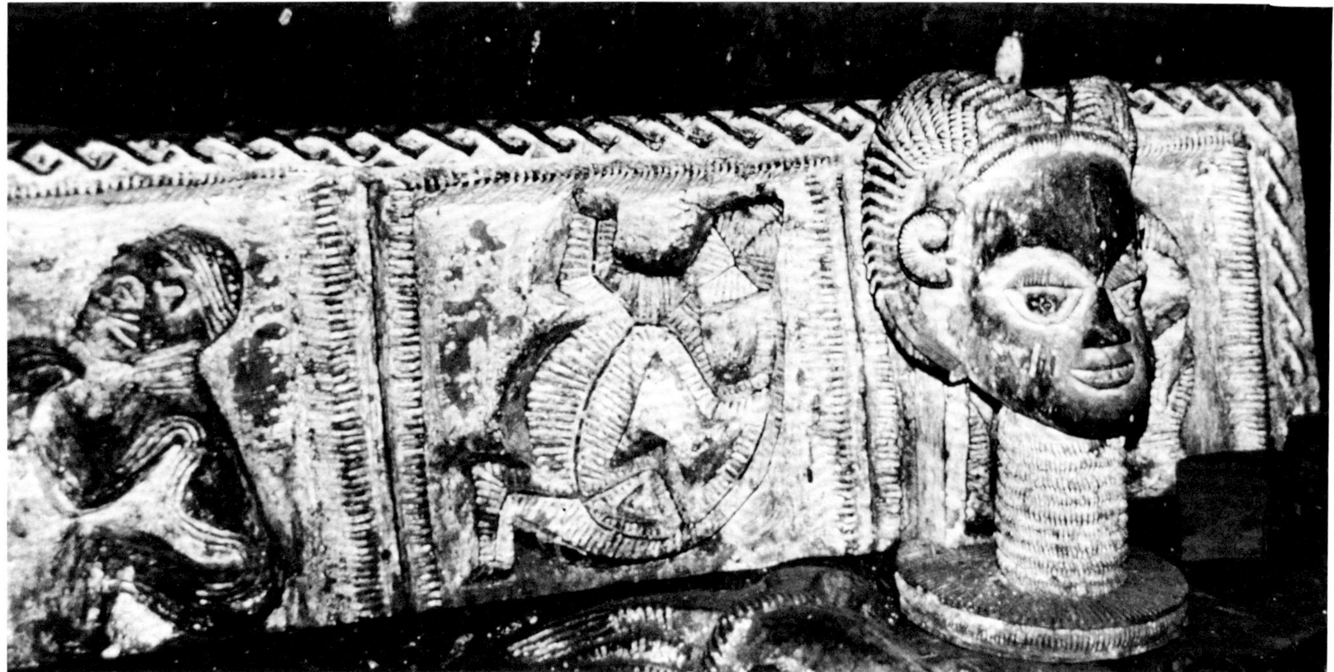

F. *Ojupo*, ancestral altar, Owo.

of the ancestors. Some represent tutelary deities with whom the family is connected, and who are honored at the time of ancestral veneration. Other objects may merely be decorations which enhance the appearance of the altar.

Often, the ancestral altar is an allusion to the power at the command of the ancestors. In Owo, altar shrines are erected over the graves of certain ancestors (see photograph F). Symbols of power abound on lintels, posts and relief sculpture found on the back and on the face of the altar. Rulers, powerful chiefs, military figures, hunters, crocodiles, leopards and elephants are all metaphors of power, alluding to the role of the ancestor both while he was living and in the afterlife. Rams' heads, roosters and catfish refer to the types of sacrifices that are made in the ancestor's honor. Beautifully carved rams' heads or human heads with horns (see photograph F) may refer to the character of the ancestor himself, for both rams and ancestors are seen as stalwart beings, patient and forgiving; yet, if angered, their wrath is terrible.

Similar shrines are erected in Ishan, north of Benin, where rams' heads are also placed on ancestral altars (see cat no. 53). Although they are different in form, the tradition of placing rams' heads on altars in Owo and Ishan apparently have a common source—Benin, where chiefs once placed such carvings on ancestral altars. Benin chiefs were later allowed the use of carved wooden human heads, more like those found on the altars of royalty.

The royal ancestral altar of Benin plays a far larger role than merely focusing on one's family's ancestors. The cult of the royal ancestor of Benin has become the state religion. The ancestral altar is the most important shrine within the palace. Bronze heads topped with exquisitely carved elephant tusks were among numerous objects placed on the altar to honor deceased rulers (see cat nos. 50, 51 and 52).[38]

The Temporal World

Although much African art is essentially religious in character, one area of African life that has encouraged the production of vast amounts of art is that of leadership. African leaders have utilized art in many ways to commemorate themselves and to work for the good of the systems they represent. Exactly how the arts of leadership and the arts of religion interrelate has not always been understood. Elsy Leuzinger, for example, has argued that

> In the areas where the king sits, godlike, upon a throne, surrounding himself with all power and worldly pomp, art ceases to be based on religion. It is no longer sacral, but decorative; instead of fulfilling a higher spiritual purpose, it serves practical needs. The monarch monopolizes it to glorify his own person and deeds . . . .[39]

However, the sacred monarch of many African kingdoms, as the visible symbol of the gods, is not glorified as a specific personality so much as his individuality is diminished in light of the *role* he plays as divine king. Kings exercise political power, given absolute authority in the past. Kings exercise economic power, formerly maintaining monopolies on trade. And, some kings exercise military power, once as warrior kings, conquering and dominating vast expanses of territory.

Art forms do, in fact, bolster the political, economic and military roles of the king and glorify him as a powerful individual. But more important than the temporal responsibilities assigned the king are his ritual tasks as intermediary between his people and the sources of power. It is through him that power for increased fertility, well-being and success are assured. Consequently, the king is, by all means, a religious figure who serves as a channel through whom vital energies can flow to enrich the lives of those he governs.

In some parts, the ritual role of the monarch as a bringer of life is his only role. As the channel of life-force controlling the fertility of crops, animals and humans, the king's personal health and well-being reflect on his kingdom. If he is not strong, the people as a whole suffer.

Many steps are taken to present the king as an uncommon being, one whose religious role as spiritual intermediary is assured by his carefully trained entourage. He is kept away from the masses, isolated within a palace. Too sacred to be ogled by the rank and file, he may be seen dimly through curtains or perhaps through a mysterious veil of cloth or fringe of beads that covers his face. Protocol is rigid, and special ritual must be observed when subjects approach the king.

Reverential treatment of kings as almost divine personages is connected to the supposition of divine descent. Genealogies are often traced to specific gods. Yoruba obas and the king of Benin trace their ancestry to Oduduwa, the creator of dry land and the first ruler of the Yoruba holy city of Ile-Ife.

Sacred kings and chiefs perform rituals, some daily, that assure their subjects' prosperity. The King of Benin, for example, occupies himself as the titular head of all religious cults in his kingdom. In addition to regular rituals which assure the health and prosperity of his people, he must perform an annual cycle of royal ceremonies which protect and purify the nation.

Much of the art of divine kingship is prestige art, whose purpose is to bolster the authority of the king and to enhance his status as ruler. These objects function to make the king and his entourage special figures.

Expansive architectural structures may be embellished by reliefs, by elaborately carved wooden doors and panels (see cat no. 37) and veranda posts (see cat nos. 4 and 5). These are sometimes covered with iconographic motifs which refer to the power and authority of the ruler or chief or to exploits in which he has been involved.

The palace is usually the hub of the community. In fact, in Yoruba towns, it is located in the center of town. The Yoruba palace may become what G.J.A. Ojo calls a "temple of temples," for in it are temples, shrines and sacred courtyards where the most important rituals of the community are performed.[40] The architecture that surrounds the monarch extends his "space" into a large portion of the capital. It is larger than the houses of any other persons in the community.

Within the palace, devices may be used to raise the king symbolically and literally above his subjects. His throne may be placed on a dais so that his position is actually higher than anyone else's. His seat of office is traditionally larger and more elaborately made than that of any of his subjects, who, in his presence, will prostrate themselves or kneel.

Other regalia may be used to call attention to the space which the king occupies. Large umbrellas become quasi-architectural devices, serving as portable architecture on the rare occasions when the king leaves the protective precincts of the palace.

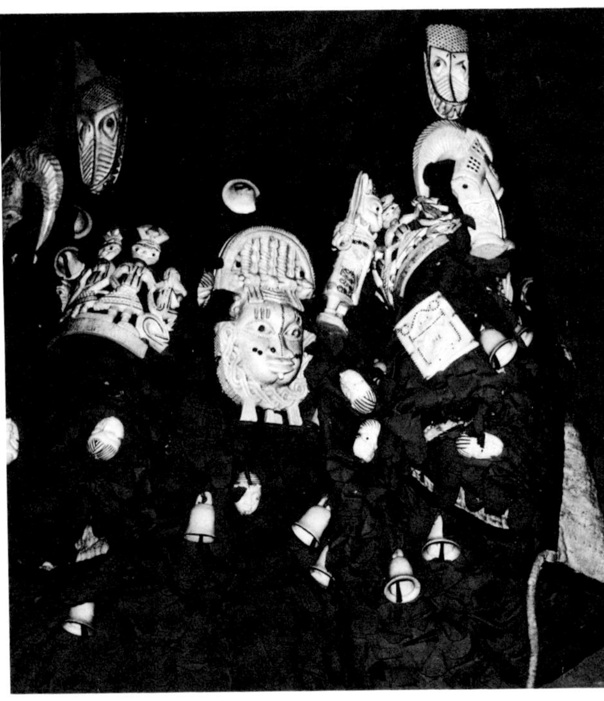

G. The *orufonran* costume of the Ojomo of Owo.

The body space of the king may be expanded by voluminous robes or wrappings of cloth (see photographs C, G). Towering crowns (see cat nos. 1, 2 and 3) or turbans may extend his height far above that of his tallest subject. Special garb may not only extend the space of the king or chief but also may make symbolic power statements. The crowns of Yoruba rulers refer both to the powers of ancestors and to those of the gods and witches. As intermediary, the king can reach and to some extent control these forces for his people. Prestige and power materials may be used to make statements about privileged position and status as well as about power. In some instances, the materials themselves may possess power. In Benin, for example, coral is said to have the power of *ase*, (similar to the Yoruba ashe) which means that whatever is said over it will come to pass.[41]

The *orufonran* costume worn by high-ranking officials in Owo is a moving sculpture gallery of power symbols cast in brass or carved in ivory (see photograph G) referring to the mystical, political and military superiority of its wearer. Made of layers of scalloped red wool fabric, itself imported and expensive, its bulkiness adds to the body space of its wearer. The imbricated layers suggest the skin of the spiny anteater, which, when it rolls itself into a ball, is invincible, protected by its spiny shell. The costume alludes, then, to the power and invincibility of its wearer through its form, its material and its iconography.

The king's power may be further alluded to by the objects he or his attendants carry. Scepters, staffs, axes, swords, fans, fly whisks and metal and ivory ornaments of all sorts are carried as symbols of office. These, too, bear motifs that are metaphors for power, but they may also carry within them mystical powers of their own.

Kings, Chiefs and Ancestors

Kings and chiefs maintain special relationships with the ancestral powers, for they serve as intermediaries with ancestors whose powers are greater than those of lesser families. Ceremonies in which the royal dead are installed as ancestors may be emphasized by artistic forms as the ako figure in Owo and Benin, (see photograph E). The altars to chiefly ancestors are accentuated in Owo (see photograph F), Ishan (see cat no. 53) and Benin, by the wooden heads of rams or humans.

Royal ancestral altars may be still more elaborate than those of chiefs and differ in size, shape and materials used. In Benin, where the royal ancestors work for the welfare of the nation as a whole, brass heads (see cat no. 50) refer to the mystic power of the head to direct life successfully. These ancestral shrines are the major shrines in the Benin palace and thus in the Benin kingdom.

Other Art Forms Supportive of Traditional Authority

In addition to art forms controlled by the palace, there are objects used by individuals, or more often, by groups which help to reinforce the traditional powers held by the aristocracy. Two examples illustrate this. In Benin, Olokun is the god of the oceans. He is the provider of children, the giver of riches, good fortune and health. His followers create elaborate shrines in his honor which contain great numbers of life-size mud images to represent him in his underwater court, attended by musicians, soldiers, chiefs, wives and an assortment of courtiers. Olokun, as the ruler of the watery realm of the ocean, is the counterpart of the oba. Art forms which depict Olukun as ruler of the spiritual hierarchy reinforce the position of the oba as the ruler of the human hierarchy.[42]

The *Epa* masquerade in northeastern Yorubaland serves to reinforce traditional values of leadership. John Pemberton III interprets them as being "celebrations of Yoruba cultural values in the context of remembering and honoring events and personages in the history of a particular community."[43] The elaborate superstructures (see cat no. 47) represent idealized types such as chiefs of hunters, mothers with children symbolizing the power of women, warriors and kings. A number of these display royal iconography. In addition, there are those that represent leopards, obvious references to royal symbolism. Epa serves to affirm and reinforce the great cultural institutions of the Yoruba such as divine kingship.

Leaders and Negative Powers

Because the king or chief has great powers at his disposal, he also has the power to counter the ravages of ominous forces which attack his subjects. The rituals the king performs may serve to cleanse his kingdom of such evil. The role of the divine king in dealing with witchcraft has already been discussed. Yet, it is not always witchcraft power that concerns the powerful. Because kings and chiefs live and act in a politically charged arena, they are often embroiled in struggles for temporal power.

Karin Barber, in her research in Okuku in Oyo state, suggests that

> Yoruba cosmology presents a picture of man, a solitary individual, picking his way . . . between a variety of forces, some benign, some hostile, many ambivalent, seeking to placate them and ally himself with them in an attempt to thwart his rivals and enemies in human society.[44]

Such human enemies might, in fact, use supernatural means to work against the man of high standing. In such contentious circumstances, the "big man" must attempt rising above

> the malicious attacks of jealous rivals and at the same time getting away with any attacks he may make on them. He was seen as an isolated individual pitted against his enemies who strove day and night to undo him. No one could be trusted.[45]

Since no human can really be trusted, other means must be employed to neutralize evil powers. Medicines and charms are placed at doorways, in courtyards and in houses. Figures may be created to house tutelary spirits which are called into service as protective agents. In Owo, protective figures may be made of clay (see photograph H) and built into a wall in the courtyard.

The Art of Overt Power

Although the first duty of divine kings was to act as intermediary with the spirit world, one must not lose sight of the fact that kingdoms and dynasties were able to continue and to expand because of military might. Great warrior kings are especially remembered by the Bini, who eventually expanded their control far into central Nigeria and along the coast to what is now the Republic of Benin.

Among the Yoruba, the Oyo kingdom organized an army that consisted of about 100,000 soldiers. Oyo dominance was felt by most Yoruba kingdoms, and with it spread military motifs in art. The horse as an awesome military machine in the early days of expansion became a symbol of power.[46] The equestrian figure is a dominant symbol in the architectural decoration of kings and chiefs.

Military power is not limited, of course, to centralized kingdoms. In areas where such governments did not exist, there were often warrior societies. In the Cross River area, very powerful men's associations organized and supervised masked performances following battles. Fantastic skin-covered masks (see cat nos. 82 and 83) may have derived from performances after battle in which actual trophy-heads were used.[47]

Art and the Powers of Social Control

Temporal power may be wielded by powerful associations of men which are sanctioned by tradition. One such organization is the Yoruba *Ogboni* society. Although it is a religious cult dedicated to the worship of Onile, the personification of earth, it is also a powerful political and judicial agent. The power of Ogboni is controlled by a few elders who serve as a judging council in matters which concern bloodshed, an offense against the earth. In many instances, it acted as a checks and balances system for the monarchy. Several art forms are used in the administering of justice and in the controlling of the various elements within society. Best known are the paired brass images of male and female figures connected by a chain, which are sent to houses of important men who have gone beyond the limits of their privilege or to houses where offenders are believed to be hiding (see cat no. 8). When the brass figures are placed in the earth, such parties must be turned over to the Ogboni. Brass images of the earth's spirit herself are said to be used to invoke the spirit to ensure the oaths of secrecy.

Many other art forms in Nigeria are used to attain some degree of social control over a group. Figures among the Mumuye (see cat no. 91) are used to detect thieves. The Igala use a special mask in an essentially judicial role in both civil and criminal cases. The

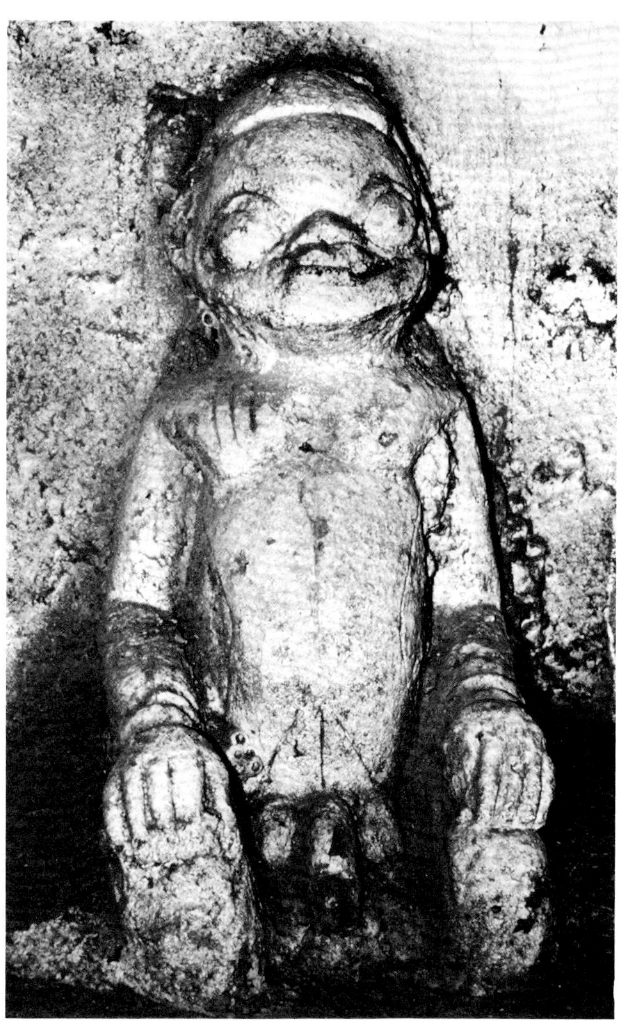

H. Protective figure in chief's compound, Owo.

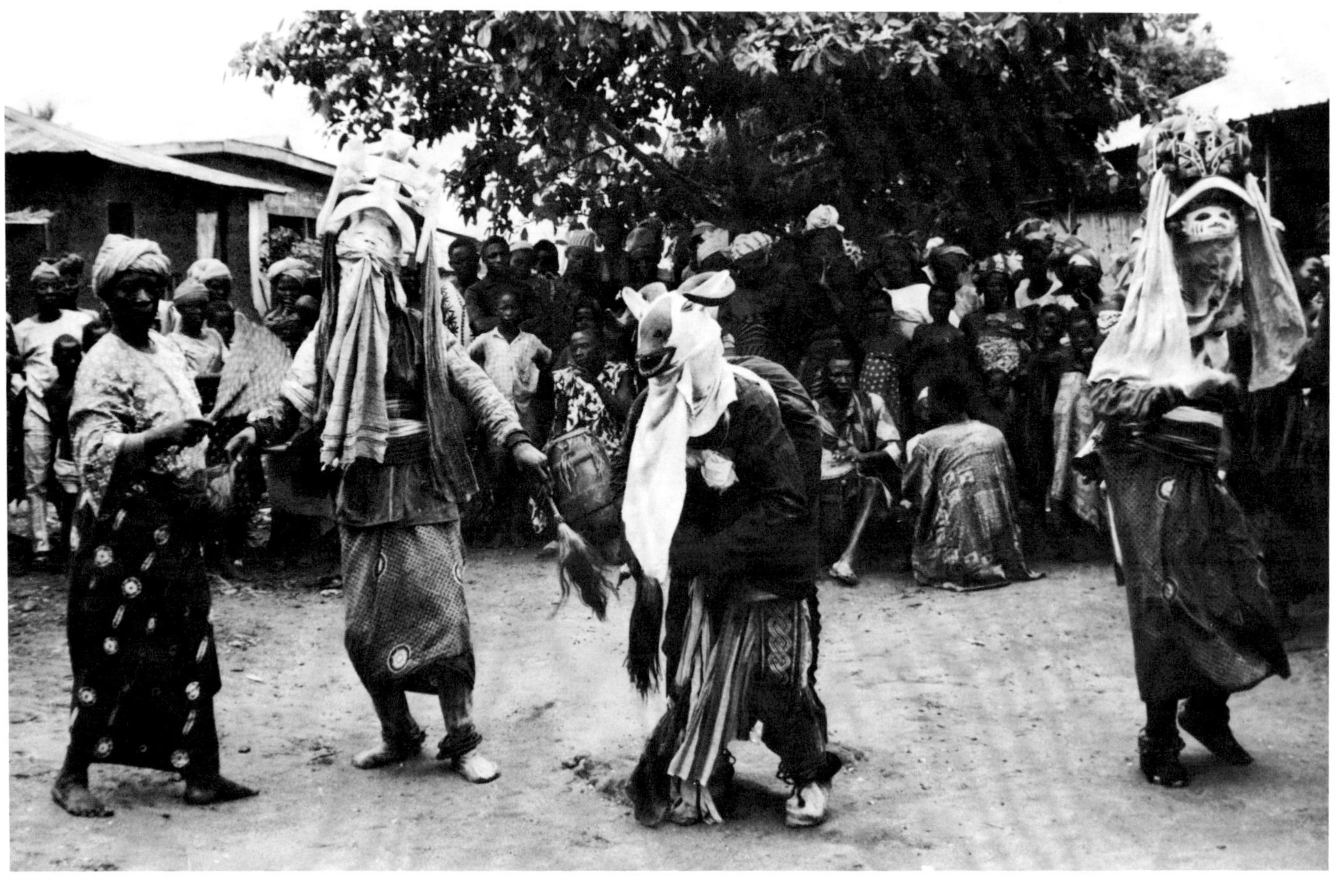

I. Gelede masked dance, Meko.

Vara society among the Chamba and the *Mangam* society among the Mama employ masks as agents of social control (see cat nos. 98 and 99).

The Etsako of southeastern Nigeria utilize masks to control social activities in both direct and indirect ways. Daytime masquerades, like Okakagbe (see cat no. 55), help promote goodwill and to minimize antisocial feelings. They generally contribute to social control by promoting community solidarity. Nighttime masquerades, on the other hand, perform social control functions through cursing thieves, seizing property of guilty parties and punishing those who commit offenses. Their role is to castigate antisocial activities within the community.[48]

Masquerade groups of the Igbo, such as those using the Afikpo *Okumkpa* play (see cat nos. 71, 72 and 73), satirize and ridicule those guilty of immoral or antisocial acts. Leaders who do not lead properly, those who act foolishly and those who do not maintain proper relative roles of masculinity and femininity are subject to censure by the masks.[49]

The *Ekon* drama association of the Ibibio employs a number of art forms, including masks and puppets, in complex performances in which they present a positive commentary on society in the presentation of idealized social types. Skits and songs in which family and social tensions are represented, depict rivalries, controversies, scandals, etc. Although individuals are directly censored by the Ekon puppets, the themes of the puppet plays and the masquerades are usually of a more general nature, dealing with political corruption, sexual mores, legal absurdities, religious frauds and excesses. Through such theatrical presentations, young men are able to criticize their elders without fear of reprisals.[50] Thus, like the Okumkpa masquerade, the Ekon association uses art in a humorous way to influence social attitudes and to bring about desired changes within the community.

Societal activities can thus be manipulated by art forms in direct ways through such organizations as Ogboni or through the influence of humor and ridicule in the activities or groups such as Ekon.

Art and Personal Power

There are channels through which the individual may assert his own personal distinctiveness and think of himself as an achiever, an entity, and not just an insignificant element in the greater reality of the social structure or the cosmos. For example, R. E. Bradbury speaks of two "cults" in Benin dedicated to aspects of a person's individuality: the Head, which symbolizes "life and behaviour in this world, the capacity to organize one's actions in such a way as to survive and prosper"; and the Hand, which is a symbol of wealth and social achievement of the individual.[51]

Both head and hand have to do with temporal success and achievement. Shrines to the head are made by powerful Bini chiefs in their private chambers. Carved wooden heads exactly like those used on chiefly ancestral altars represent the successful life of the chief as expressed in his destiny, his good head.[52]

The concept of the head as the locus of destiny is shared by the Yoruba. The head is honored by some Yoruba with an object made as a miniature cowry-covered crown. The "head" made in this manner is given a "house," also made to resemble a crown (see cat no. 7).

Destiny is not something, however, that has been handed out and over which the individual has no control. Both the Yoruba and the Edo believe that the individual, before birth, appears before the High God and determines his own fate, which he proceeds to live out on earth.

The hand is not associated so much with fate in Benin thought as it is with the individual's personal will and self-determination. When one has led a prosperous life, he may choose to erect an altar to his own hand (see cat no. 54). The shrine to the hand, *ikegobo*, expedites the ritual expression of self-esteem and self-congratulations.

Personal shrines which relate to achievement and to male assertiveness are found over a large area of southern Nigeria. J. S. Boston's research suggests that the Igbo *ikenga* "symbolizes the person as a particular individual, contrasting his own personal achievements with those which can be ascribed to hereditary qualities or to some other external source."[53] Competitiveness and preoccupation with personal achievement among the Igbo make the cult of the hand almost ubiquitous in Igbo country. The ikenga, like its Benin counterpart, is associated with the power of the owner's right arm (see cat nos. 59 and 60).

Not all personal power shrines are associated specifically with the hand. The Urhobo, the Isoko and the Ijo of southern Nigeria all have artistic forms dedicated to what might be considered personality traits. The Isoko, according to Phil Peek, sometimes consider *ivri* to be a deity, but more often it is the quality of "adamance, tenacity sometimes becoming stubbornness."[54] A person who has too much ivri must obtain a small carving to help control that aspect of his personality. Likewise, the *ivwri* of the Urhobo go beyond the concept of personal achievement to deal with the concepts of aggression and retribution. Perkins Foss suggests that one's aggressive potential is controlled and channeled through the image. It helps to establish peaceful coexistence in Urhobo society, establishing equilibrium.[55]

The world is a complex of powers, both supernatural and visible. These powers can be controlled through proper ritual which comes through knowledge and training. Ritual is the bridge that connects the powers of the visible and the invisible worlds, and it is sculpture, along with word, substance, music and dance, that makes ritual visible and meaningful.

Robin Poynor, PhD, University of Florida

1 McNaughton, 1979. pp. 24-25.
2 Nadel, 1954. pp. 13-15.
3 Ubah, 1982. p. 92.
4 Drewal and Drewal, 1983, p.6
5 Cole, 1969 c.p. 39.
6 Siroto, 1976. p. 8.
7 Prince, 1961. pp. 796-7.
8 Ibid.
9 Morton-Williams, 1961. p. 247.
10 Poynor, 1978. p. 76.
11 Drewal and Drewal, 1983. p. 8.
12 Arinze, 1970. pp. 17-20.
13 Ibid. pp. 55-58.
14 Kopytoff, 1971. p. 129.
15 Cole, 1969 c. pp. 39-40.
16 Horton, 1965. p. 8.
17 Ibid. p. 10.
18 Ibid. p. 15.
19 Foss, 1976, pp. 179, 197.
20 Cole, 1969 a, p. 8.
21 See Cole 1969 a, 1969 b, 1982.
22 M.Drewal, 1977. p. 43.
23 Wescott, 1962. pp. 345-8.
24 Fagg and Pemberton, 1982. p. 100.
25 Barber, 1981. p. 725.
26 Fagg and Pemberton, 1982. p. 156.
27 Siroto, 1976. p. 14.
28 Borgatti, 1979. pp. 4, 5, 10.
29 Ibid. p. 7.
30 Thompson, 1972, pp. 245-56.
31 Ibid. p. 253.
32 Ibid.
33 Drewal and Drewal, 1983. p. 162.
34 Ibid. p. 220.
35 Blier, 1976. pp. 4, 5.
36 Murray, 1947. p. 313.
37 See Siroto, 1976.
38 Ben-Amos, 1980. p. 64.
39 Leuzinger, 1967. p. 34.
40 Ojo, 1966b. p. 76.
41 Ben-Amos, 1980. p. 68.
42 Ibid.
43 Fagg and Pemberton, 1982. p. 72.
44 Barber, 1981. p. 729.
45 Ibid.
46 Ojo, 1966 a, p. 121.
47 Blier, 1980. p. 13.
48 Borgatti, 1979. p. 5.
49 Ottenberg, 1975. pp. 129-38.
50 Scheinberg, 1977. np.
51 Bradbury, 1973. p. 262.
52 Ben-Amos, 1980. p. 60.
53 Boston, 1977. p. 14.
54 Peek, 1981. pp. 140, 142. in Vogel, 1981.
55 Foss, 1976. p. 76.

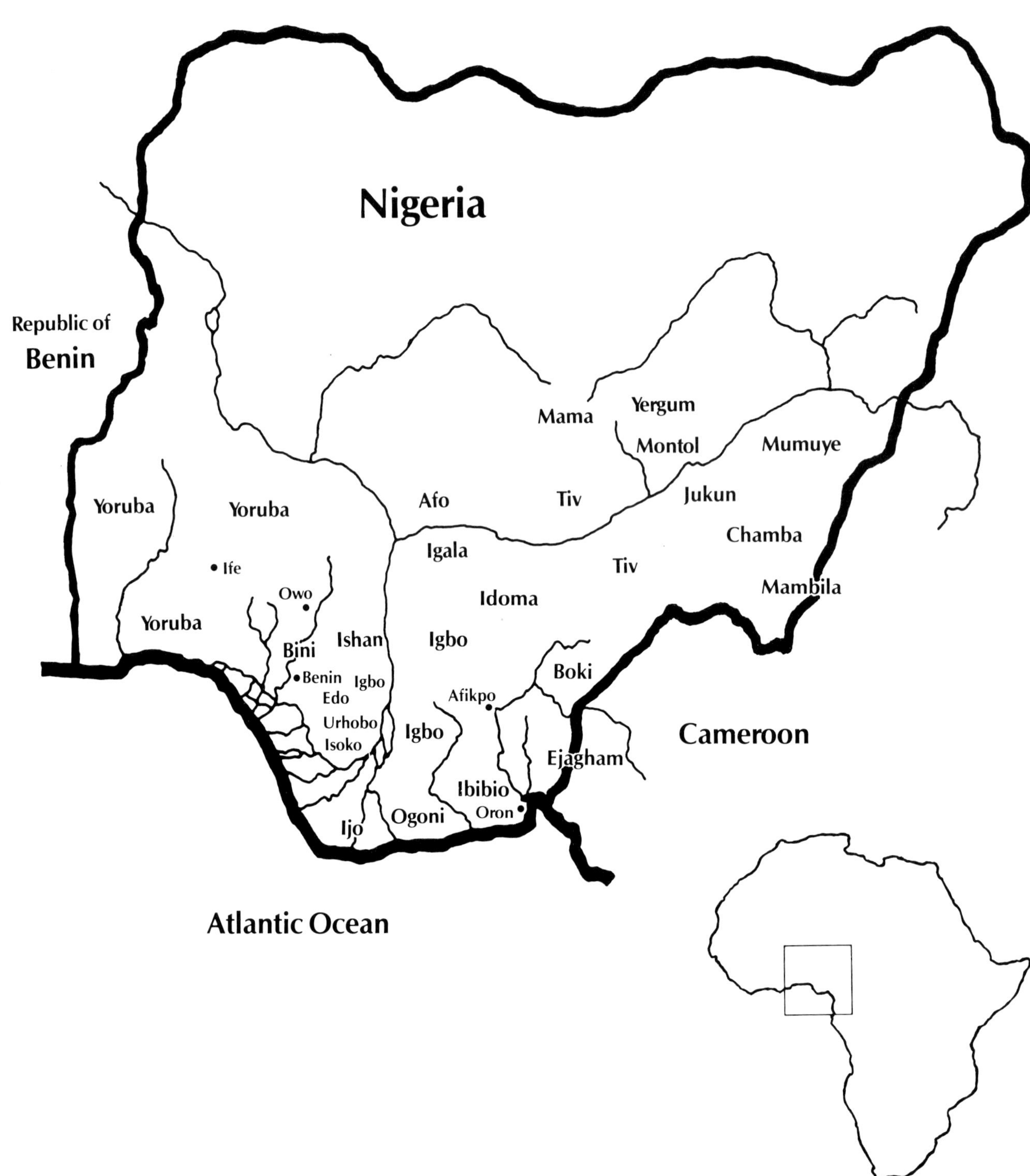
Nigeria
Republic of
Benin
Mama
Yergum
Montol
Mumuye
Yoruba
Yoruba
Afo
Tiv
Jukun
Chamba
Igala
Tiv
Ife
Owo
Idoma
Mambila
Yoruba
Bini
Ishan
Igbo
Boki
Benin
Igbo
Edo
Afikpo
Urhobo
Isoko
Igbo
Cameroon
Ejagham
Ibibio
Oron
Ijo
Ogoni
Atlantic Ocean

NIGERIA

Diversity is the overriding characteristic of the climate, geography and peoples of Nigeria. Over 140 inches of rainfall a year drench the far south where mangrove swamps are a prominent feature of the Niger River Delta. In the north, savanna grasslands provide a grazing area for cattle of nomadic herders. Rainfall decreases to under thirty inches a year in the far north, and vegetation becomes sparser. The peoples of Nigeria form a complex mosaic of ethnic affiliations. Over eighty million people, one-fourth of all Africans, inhabit Nigeria's 350,000 square miles and are members of several hundred ethnic groups.

The concept of Nigeria as a unit is recent and dates from the colonial and post-colonial periods. Like many African nations, Nigeria's political boundaries are the result of decisions made by Europeans in the nineteenth century and did not develop from internal ethnic and cultural affinities. Nigeria was first considered an entity in 1914 when the British protectorates of Northern and Southern Nigeria were joined under a single governorship. Independent nationhood came in 1960 after nearly one hundred years of British rule. As might be expected from the history of this continent, cultural identity and ethnic affiliation in many parts of Africa often transcend national borders. Nigerian examples of this include the Mambila people who live on both sides of the Nigeria-Cameroon border as do many Cross River groups. Likewise, Yorubaland extends into the Republic of Benin and Togo.

Nigeria's artistic heritage is one of great antiquity. Sophisticated terra cotta sculptures have been dated to the first millenium B.C. Ancient objects made of wood and more perishable materials decayed long ago, but examples made of durable media such as brass, copper or clay remain. Works from Nok, Igbo Ukwu, Ife, Owo and Benin (cat nos. 48, 49, 50, 51, 52) attest to rich traditions of plastic arts. Distinct associations with power have been suggested for these earlier works.[1] Human representations in ancient art range from the highly naturalistic to the geometric to the fantastic and grotesque. While including a few pieces to represent these older traditions, this exhibition will concentrate on works less than one hundred years old.

Traditional sculpture which is closely tied to indigenous religious beliefs continues to be produced in some areas although it is no longer made in others. Sometimes its use persists in a secularized manner or in conjunction with non-traditional religious practices. Today, the northern region of Nigeria is predominately Islamic while Christianity dominates the south. Most people of the smaller ethnic groups in the middle section practice traditional religions though many are Christians. Essays and entries are written in the present tense even though many of the objects are no longer made and the beliefs and practices which inspired them are no longer held.

The stylistic pluralism in Nigerian art can be seen in the works included in this exhibition which range from the simple pole-like abstract form of a Chamba figure (cat no. 89) to the almost uncanny naturalism of an Ejagham headcrest (cat no. 82). Visual relationships among sculptural styles reflect a general rule that similar stylistic traits in the arts of Africa tend to be found among ethnically and culturally related peoples.

The catalog of the works in this exhibition is organized by ethnic grouping. In the entries, the name of the large ethnic division appears in bold type; subgroup and area designation follow.

Works are twentieth century unless indicated otherwise. Unless a specific source is cited, population and general ethnographic information are from Murdock (1959) and Bascomb (1973).

1 See Ben Amos, Eyo & Willett, Ben Amos & Rubin, ed. for discussion of power associations of ancient Nigerian art.

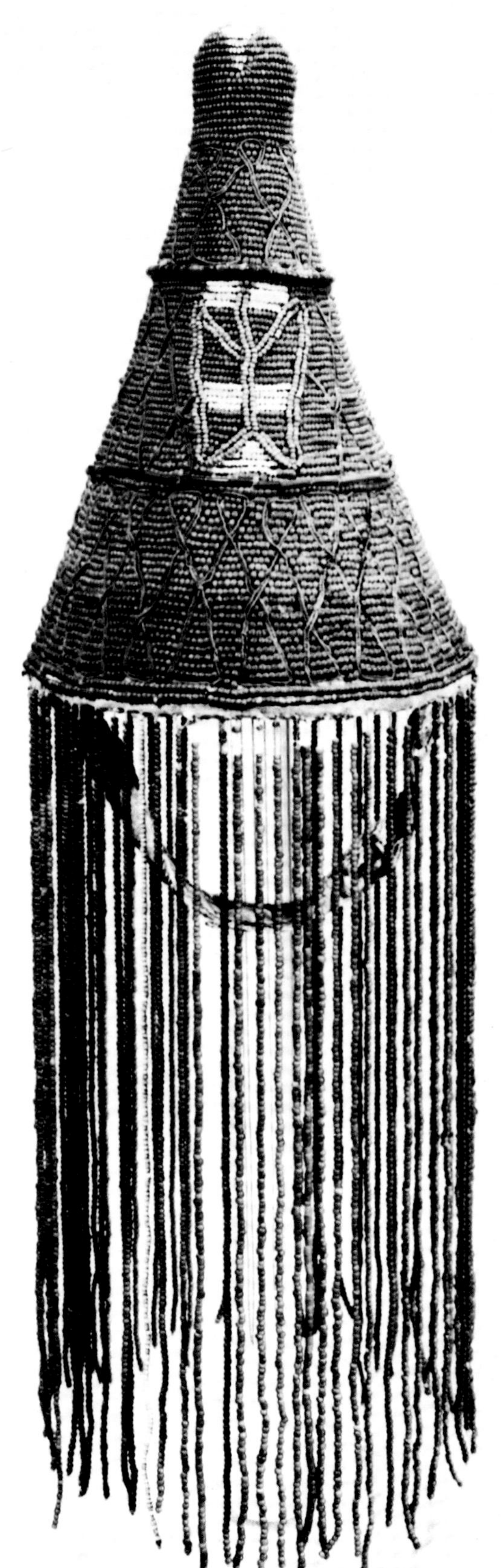

2

Yoruba

The Yoruba (population 10,000,000) live in southwestern Nigeria and are considered Africa's most prolific sculptors. For centuries they have been an urban people. The Yoruba developed a system of autonomous city-states ruled by powerful kings. The original sixteen kingdoms are said to have been founded by the sons and grandsons of Oduduwa, the divine founder of the holy city of Ife where, the Yoruba believe, human life began. Despite local variation, Yoruba art and culture show great homogeneity. Indigenous religion involves belief in a distant creator god and the worship of numerous deities (*orisha*).

1. BEADED CROWN(*ADE*)
Yoruba, Ijebu
Glass beads, fiber, h. 28″
The Milton D. Ratner Family Collection

According to one widely held Yoruba tradition, the city of Ife is the site where land was first created by the orisha Oduduwa who descended from heaven on a golden chain. Oduduwa became Ife's first king, and his sons founded the other sixteen Yoruba kingdoms. Only those rulers who can trace their genealogy back to Oduduwa have the right to wear the beaded veiled crown and beaded slippers and possess the other beaded acoutrements that are the insignia of the divine kings of Yorubaland.

The crown contains powerful medicines to protect the king and to enhance his spiritual and temporal powers. The crown itself is called an orisha, a god. Beaded birds refer to "the mothers" (see cat no. 39) without whose protection the king cannot rule. In their destructive aspect, the mothers are witches who can transform themselves into birds of the night and devour their victims. The hierarchal arrangement of birds may also refer to the structure of Yoruba government, and the number of birds on a single crown may have symbolic references. The zigzag pattern symbolizes both snakes and lightning.

Drewal, 1977. p. 12, ill. cat no. 3.
Thompson, 1970. pp. 16-17.
Thompson, 1976. CH 8/1-3
Fagg, 1980. pp. 9-15. (Pemberton, p. 50.)

2. BEADED CROWN (*ADENLA*)
Yoruba
Glass beads, fiber, h. 41″
The Milton D. Ratner Family Collection

The great bird at the top of this *adenla* (great crown) is attached by a peg to the concealed medicines inside. According to Robert Thompson, this bird may refer to the defeat of the witches by the god of divination using the force of his superior intellect. The frontal face which suggests ancestral power can also be read as the head of an elephant, a common royal symbol. Interlacing designs which also appear on this crown have ancient associations with kingship.

Fagg, 1980. ill., pl. 24. (Pemberton p. 78.)
Thompson, 1976. CH 8/1-2.

3. BEADED CROWN (*ADE*)
Yoruba
Beads, fiber, h. 28½″
The Milton D. Ratner Family Collection

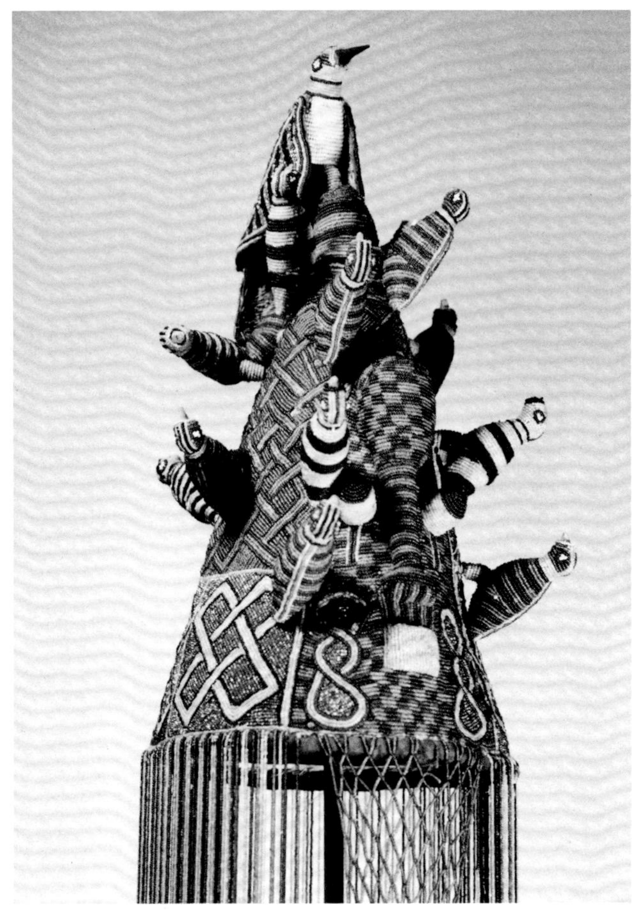

3

The use and manufacture of beads and their association with kingship were important long before tiny trade beads of European origin became available in the nineteenth century. There was a bead-making industry at Ife during the classical period (A.D. 1000-1500), and beads, some of which were painted red, have been found attached to the bronze heads excavated there. Red cornelian and coral beads are thought to have been important in the royal arts of the Yoruba in the sixteenth to eighteenth centuries as well as in the royal arts of Benin.

Fagg, 1980. pp. 9-12. ill. p. 51, pl. 10.

4., 5. PAIR OF VERANDA POSTS
Yoruba, Ekiti, Efon-Alaiye
Wood, pigment h. 79", 80"
The Milton D. Ratner Family Collection

Traditional Yoruba architecture consists of a compound built to house an extended family. This compound is constructed around an open impluviam courtyard which contains a wide veranda used for many purposes. The palaces of kings, compounds of important members of society and the shrines of orisha are distinguished by elaborately carved, figurative veranda posts on which appear many of the themes seen in other examples of Yoruba carving.

This pair of posts is attributed by Drewal to the master carver Obembe Alaiye or his workshop and dates from the early twentieth century.

H. Drewal, 1977 p. 17-19. ill. p. 18 cat no. 10-11.
Ojo, 1968. pp. 14-17, 70-72.
Fagg and Pemberton, 1982. ill. cat no. 47, p. 42.

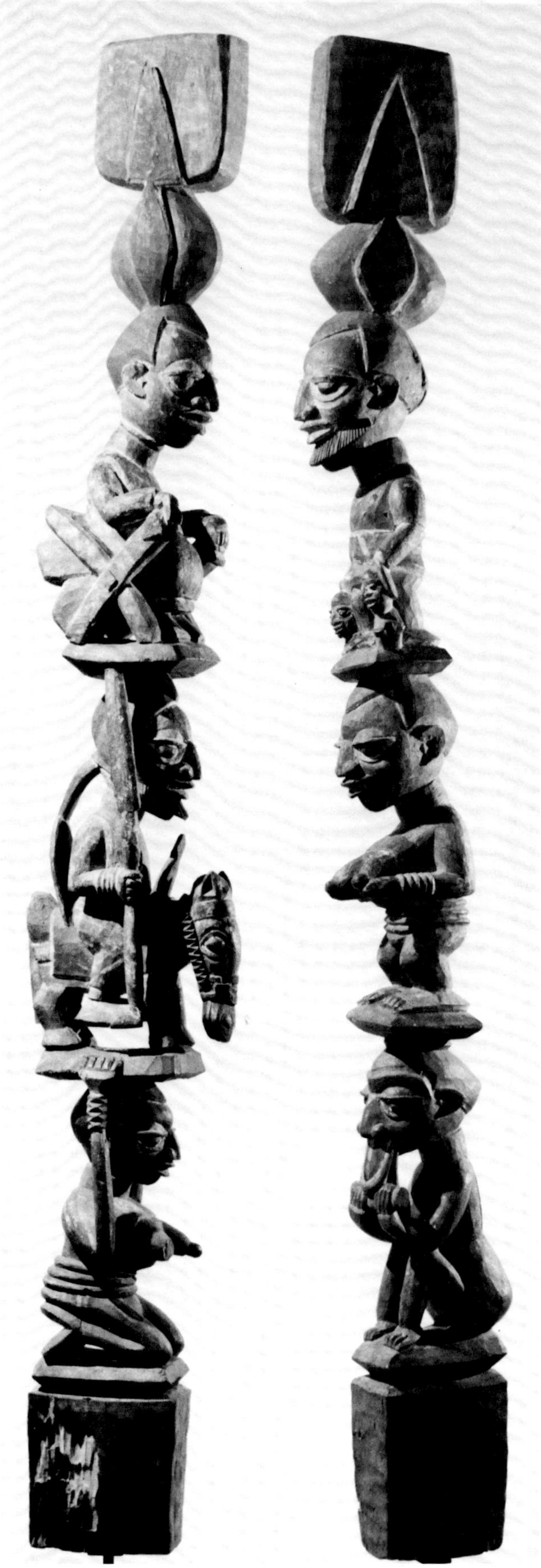

4, 5

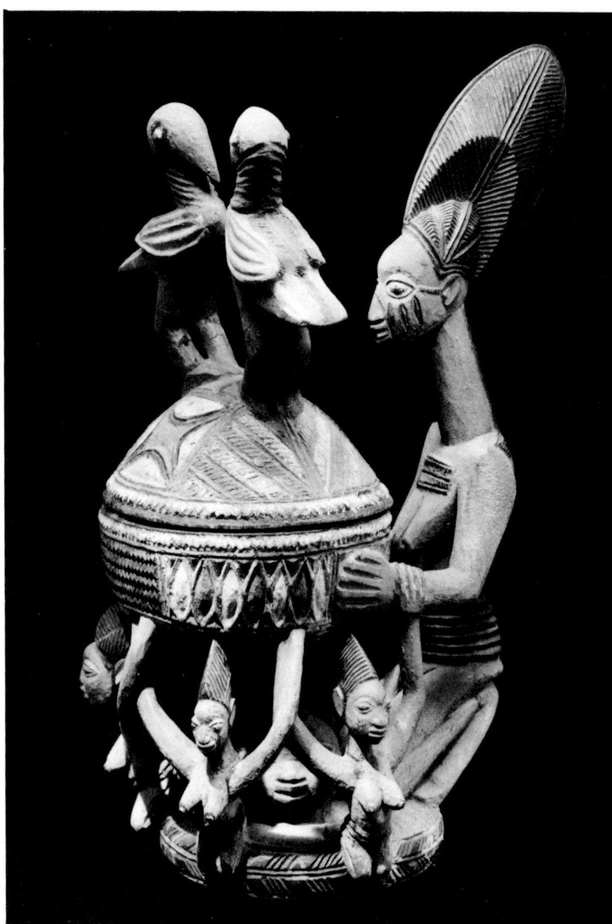

6. FIGURE WITH BOWL
Yoruba, Ekiti
Olowe of Ise
Wood, pigment, h. 21¼″
The Paul and Ruth Tishman Collection

One Western misconception about African art is that the African artist is anonymous. While it is true that in some African societies sculpture is made by non-professional or part-time artists, among the Yoruba and others sculpture is made by highly trained professionals. Since the 1930s a great deal of work has been done toward identifying the styles and names of individual carvers.

Olowe of Ise-Ekiti who died in 1938 is considered the greatest Yoruba sculptor of this century. He is best known for his architectural sculptures such as doors and houseposts, and his chief patron was the Arinjale (king) of Ise.

This elaborately carved, covered bowl was used to present kola nuts to a chief's guests or may have been used for storing equipment for Ifa divination. The head in the lower portion is carved to move freely within the space created by the supporting figures, but cannot be removed.

Fagg, in Vogel, ed., 1981. p. 104-105. ill. pl. 56.
Fagg and Pemberton, 1982. pp. 42-44.

7. HOUSE OF THE HEAD (*ILE ORI*)
Yoruba
Cowrie shells, cloth, hide, h. 13½″
Lent by Pace Gallery

To the Yoruba, the head is the container of the soul, the essence of personality, the determinant of one's fortune and one's personal sovereign. The head is honored with a crown-shaped object covered with cowrie shells. Prayers to sustain the power of the head are directed to the *ile ori*.

Thompson, 1971. CH 9/1-2.

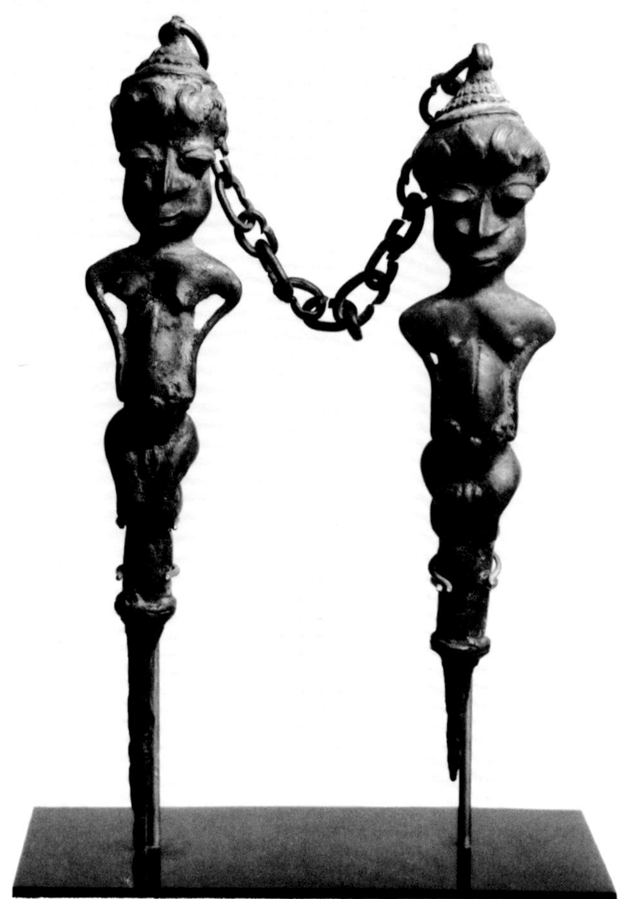

8. STAFFS (*EDAN OGBONI*)
Yoruba
Nineteenth-twentieth centuries
Bronze, h. 8″
Lent by Riccardo Salmona

The *Ogboni* (or *Oshugbo*) society is an important political and spiritual force for the Yoruba people. Elders who belong to this secret society act as powerful judges and can overrule, and even depose, a king in certain instances. Their spiritual power comes from the goddess Onile, the owner of the earth and the source of moral law. Ogboni society members are empowered with trying and punishing those who offend her.

High ranking Ogboni society members are entitled to own twinned male and female brass figures (*edan ogboni*) attached to iron rods and linked by a chain. These emblems of status and authority are sometimes worn around the neck and also have powers of social control.

Thompson, 1971. CH 6/1-2.

9. SHANGO PEDESTAL (*ODO SHANGO*)
Yoruba, Igbomina, Oro area
Wood, pigment, h. 12¼″
Lent by Dr. and Mrs. Robert Phillips

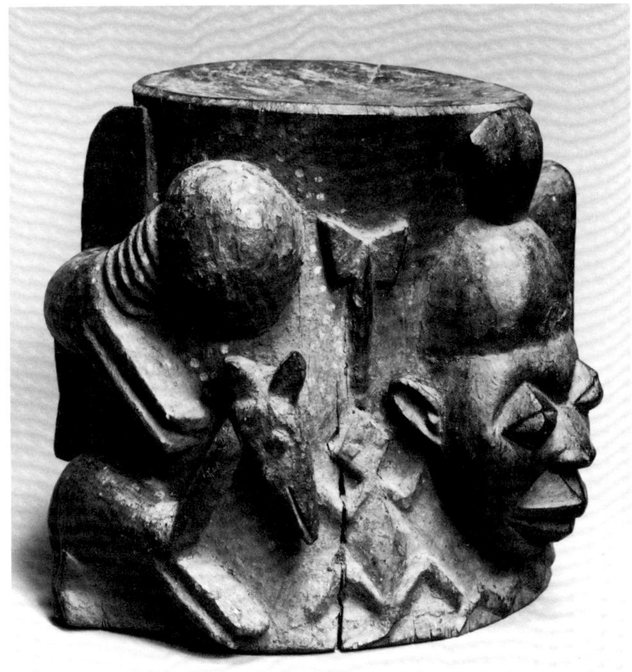

9

Shango, the unpredictable and fiery-tempered orisha of thunder and lightning, is identified with the fourth king of the ancient Yoruba state of Oyo. According to legend, Shango, the king, was a great magician who had the power to emit smoke and flames from his mouth and to produce thunder and lightning. He was exiled from Oyo for his abusive exercise of power and hanged himself. He was later deified. Like the rain, Shango, the orisha, posesses both creative and destructive powers; blessings and fertility come to his devotees while his thunder bolts cause destruction and suffering.

Many objects are used in the worship of this deity by members of the Shango cult. Worship occurs at lavish shrines which allude to Shango's royal origin. At such a shrine is placed an *odo* Shango (pedestal) in the shape of an inverted mortar used to pound yams. Such a pedestal holds a bowl in which "thunderstones" found at houses struck by lightning are placed. Odo may also be used as seats for priests or initiates of the Shango cult or may be beaten as drums.

The central image of this odo is that of a Shango priest balancing a thunderstone on his head. Surrounding him are *oshe* and animals which are mentioned in praise songs to the orisha. Snakes near the base of the pedestal are considered Shango's messengers. A *laba*, an ornamented leather bag which is the priest's badge of office, hangs to the left of his face.

Fagg and Pemberton, 1982, pp. 114-115, ill. pl. 46.
Lawal, 1971. pp. 26-29.
Thompson, 1976. Ch. 12.

10. STAFF FOR SHANGO (*OSHE SHANGO*)
Yoruba

Wood, pigment, h. 18″
Lent by Mr. and Mrs. E. M. Friend Jr.

Carved wooden staffs (*oshe*) for Shango are owned by all members of the Shango cult and are placed on their personal altars. The cult member who is possessed by the orisha dances with his or her oshe at festivals honoring Shango.

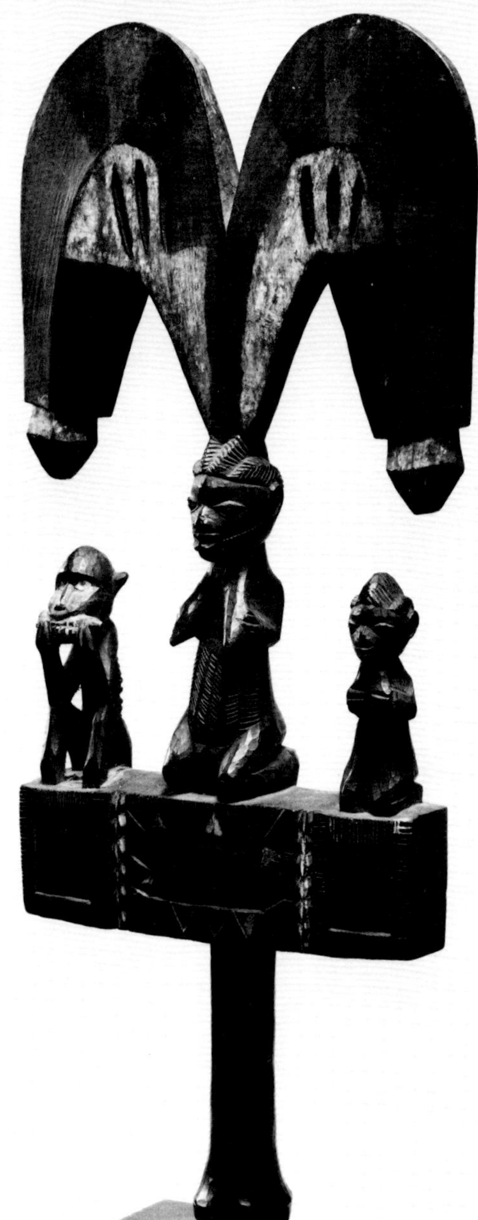

10

The oshe in its simplest form is a double-faced axe and is symbolic of the splitting power of lightning. There are many forms of oshe, and devotees may own several, each in a different style. This elaborate polychrome example contains a central kneeling figure balancing on her head the double axe form which terminates in thunderstones. She is flanked by a smaller kneeling figure who also wears the braided hairdo of a Shango worshipper and a monkey eating corn. The monkey is associated with Shango because the sacred grove where Shango hanged himself was inhabited by monkeys. The horizontal bar on which the figures rest contains a relief carving of a divination board and chains of cowrie shells which have connections with both Shango and divination. The divination board may have reference to the owner's allegiance to Shango. A person adopts a particular deity because that deity is worshipped by his mother or father or because a diviner directs him to serve that god.

Lawal, 1971. pp. 93-102.
Bascomb, 1969. pp. 77, 84.

11. STAFF FOR SHANGO (*OSHE SHANGO*)
Yoruba, Oyo, Ibadan
Wood, beads, h. 16″
Private collection

This oshe is in the style of two works in the Arnett collection attributed by Henry Drewal to the workshop or hand of the Ibadan artist Amos Lafia of Idi Aro who lived in the late nineteeth or early twentieth century. From the incised shaft emerge two rows of four small heads each and a head on either side of the double-bladed axe. Multiples of four are important in Yoruba thought and figure prominently in Ifa divination. Strings of red and white glass beads worn by Shango worshippers encircle the staff.

Drewal, 1980. p. 30. cf. pl. 15, 16.
Bascomb, 1969. pp. 70-72, 84.

12. STAFF FOR SHANGO (*OSHE SHANGO*)
Yoruba, Egba area
Wood, h. 14½″
Lent by Mr. and Mrs. Paul Kassouf

The female devotee shown on this oshe Shango balances the thunder axe and cools its fire with her calm kneeling posture.

Fagg and Pemberton, ill. p. 109, pl. 28.
Thompson, 1976. CH 12/3

13. STAFF FOR SHANGO (*OSHE SHANGO*)
Yoruba, Efon-Alaiye
Wood, h. 12″
Lent by Dr. and Mrs. Clifton Latting

Pairs of twinned heads support the double-headed thunder axe in this oshe. The thunder god has a special relationship with twins.

Thompson, 1976. CH 13/4.
Thompson, 1974. pp. 96-97.

14. STAFF FOR SHANGO (*OSHE SHANGO*)
Yoruba
Wood, h. 16¼″
Lent by Dr. and Mrs. Robert Phillips

15. STANDING SHRINE FIGURE FOR SHANGO
Yoruba, Illa-Orangun
Wood, indigo h. 15″
Private collection

This shrine figure for Shango exemplifies Yoruba aesthetic criteria as recorded by Robert Thompson. The figure is shown at the optimum of life, neither young or old. The treatment strikes a balance between abstraction and representation and shows the desired qualities of luminosity, visibility, "symmetry, positioning. . . , delicacy, relative straightness upright posture, and skill. . . ."

Thompson, 1968. pp. 63-66.

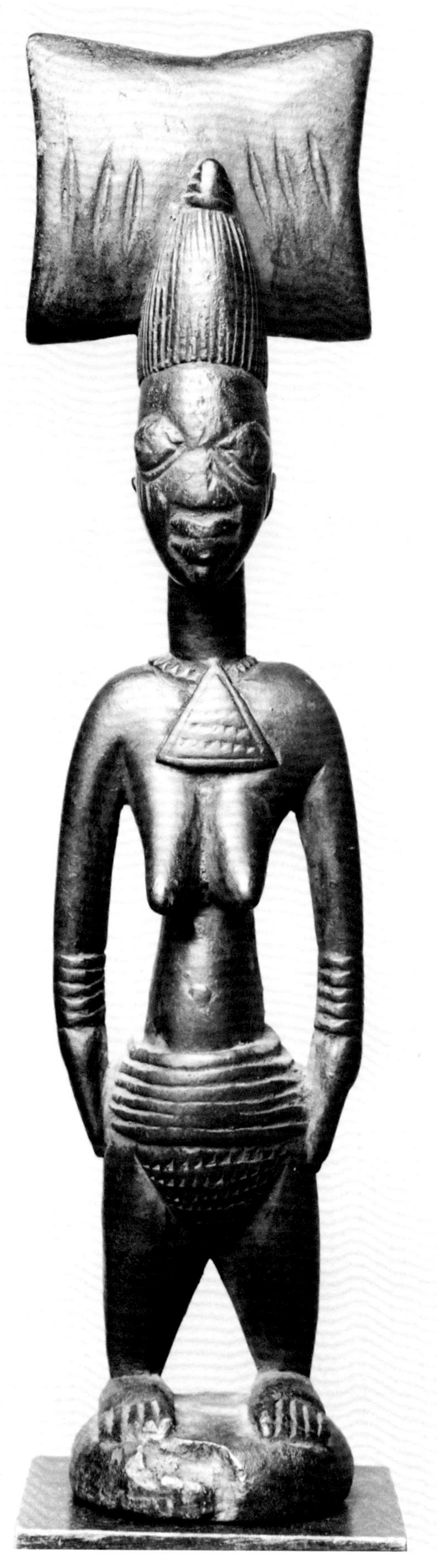

15

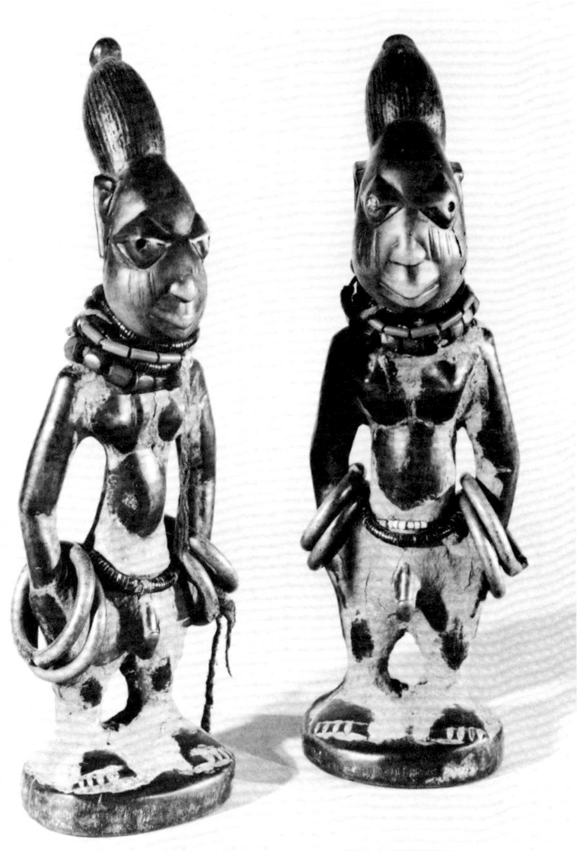

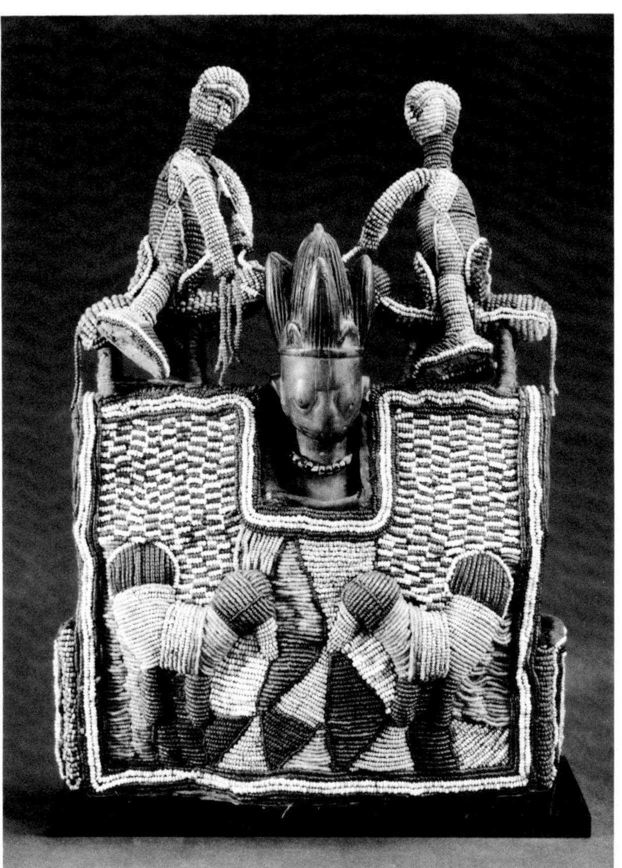

16., 17. PAIR OF TWIN FIGURES (*ERE IBEJI*)
Yoruba, Igbomina
Wood, beads, metal, h. 11″
The Milton D. Ratner Family Collection

The Yoruba have the highest rate of twinning in the world; forty-five twin births occur out of every one thousand births. This is four times the rate in the United States. Twins are believed to share a single soul and possess special powers. Twin births are extraordinary events, and twins can bring either wealth and good luck or misfortune to their families depending on how they are treated.

When one or a pair of twins dies, the parents consult a diviner who may prescribe the carving of *ere ibeji* (twin statuettes). These memorial figures are kept on a family twin altar, in the mother's sleeping room or in a storage container. They are washed, rubbed with cosmetics such as camwood and indigo, fed, danced with in the market place and given clothing and jewelry just as living twins would be. This attention insures that the twins in spirit form will continue their benevolence to their family and that future deaths of children will be prevented.

Houlberg, 1973. pp. 20-27.

18., 19. PAIR OF TWIN FIGURES (*ERE IBEJI*)
Yoruba, Igbomina, Ila
Wood, beads, metal h. 12″, 11¾″
Private collection

Twin figures from the Igbomina Yoruba of the Ila area are often carved without a base and wearing platform sandles. The triangular protective charms on front and back are of Muslim origin.

Stoll and Stoll, 1980. pp. 288-289.

20. TWIN FIGURE WITH JACKET (*ERE IBEJI*)
Yoruba
Wood, beads, h. 15½″
Nineteenth-twentieth centuries
The Paul and Ruth Tishman Collection

The beaded garment worn by this twin image probably indicates that the deceased was of royal birth. (see cat nos. 1-3, 36) A pair of birds appears in low relief on the front of the garment, and two mounted horsemen facing inward stand on the shoulders. In addition to their own symbolic power associations, these images reinforce the concept of the power of doubling inherent in the ibeji cult.

Houlberg in Vogel, ed., 1981. p. 101. ill. pl. 52.
Siroto, 1976. ill. p. 87, no. 166.

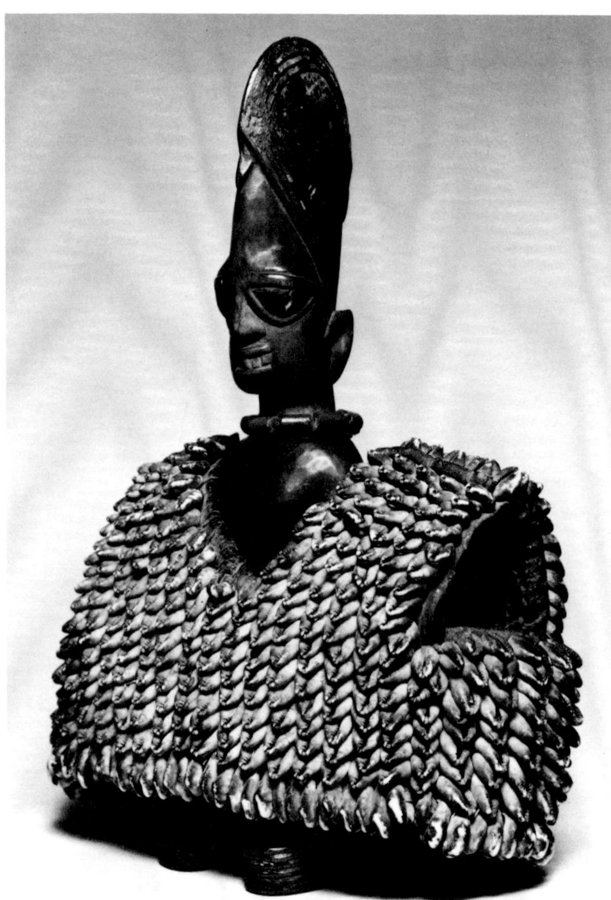

21. TWIN FIGURE (*ERE IBEJI*)

Yoruba, Igbomina
Wood, cowrie shells, fabric, beads, h. 12″
Lent by Dr. John Nixon

This twin figure is in the style of the carver Dagikonle of Ogbomole, who was active in the 1940s. The cowrie shell cloak resembles the cowrie covered garment worn by the senior priest of the thunder god, Shango. Twins are said to derive their powers from Shango, and he is considered to be their special protector.

Thompson, 1976. CH 13/3, pl. 75.

22. TWIN FIGURE (*ERE IBEJI*)

Yoruba
Wood, h. 10½″
Lent by Retina and Vitreous Associates

23. ESHU FIGURE

Yoruba, Igbomina, Idofin
Wood h. 12½″
Private collection

Eshu Elegba is the only Yoruba orisha consistently depicted in sculpted form. The messenger to the gods, he conveys to them the sacrifices and prayers of men and women. This powerful deity is also the trickster of the Yoruba pantheon and personifies the principle of uncertainty in the ordered Yoruba universe. He disrupts the lives and fortunes of humans who forget his power and, by so doing, causes them to return to proper ritual observances. This kneeling Eshu figure from Igbomina plays a flute or whistle, one of his more common attributes. The flute is both a sign of his role as a divine herald and a symbol of his socially improper and unrestrained behavior. It also alludes to his masculine vitality and phallic powers.

Fagg and Pemberton, 1982. ill. pl. 20 p. 92.
Wassing, 1968. ill. cat. 40. p. 244.

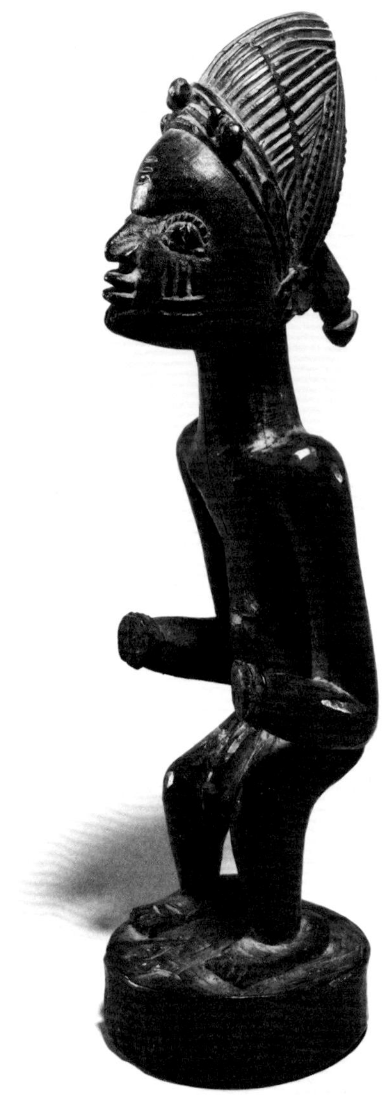

24. ESHU FIGURE

Yoruba
Wood. h. 14⅜″
Birmingham Museum of Art, gift of Margaret Pennington in honor of her mother, Mrs. Regina Kirchoff Mandrell 1984.58

This crouching Eshu figure wears the orisha's characteristic long-tailed hairdo. The phallic association of this coiffure is quite explicit in this treatment.

25. DANCE STAFF FOR ESHU

Yoruba
Wood. h. 11½″
Lent by Edward M. Friend III

Small dance staffs are held by Eshu devotees. This kneeling

female figure wears a headdress adorned with calabashes containing powerful substances. The staff is darkened with indigo as are numbers 23 and 26. Indigo is linked with wealth and power; the resulting black color has associations for the Yoruba with night and evil.

Wescott, 1962. p. 339.

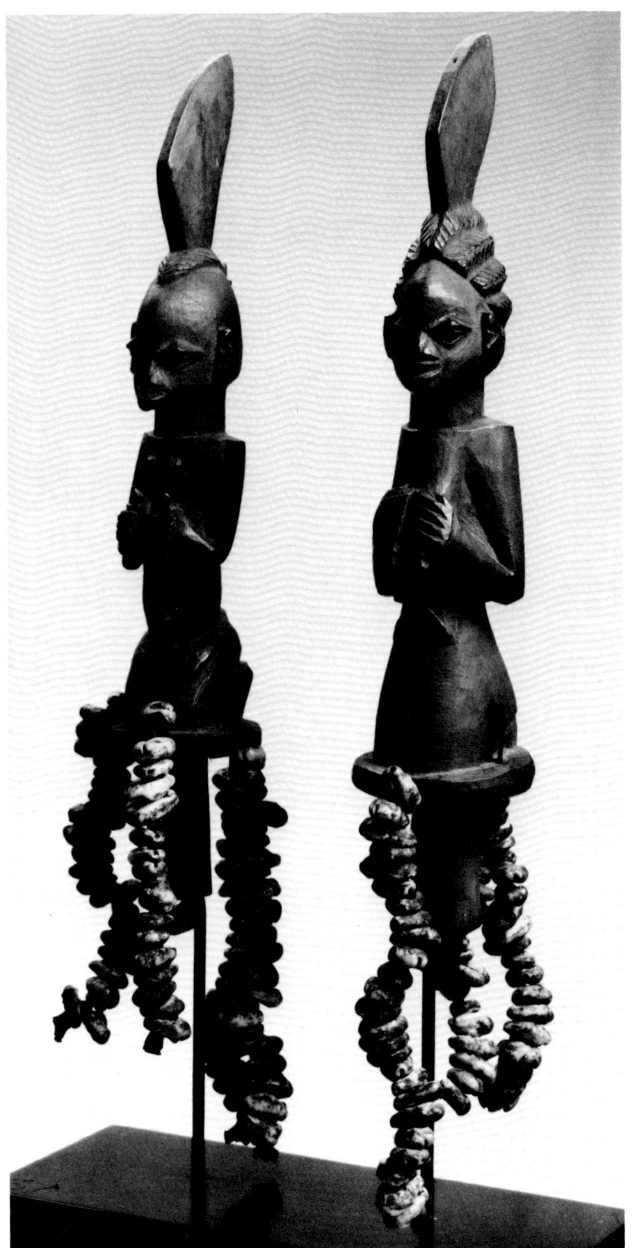

26. PAIR OF DANCE IMAGES FOR ESHU
Yoruba
Wood, cowrie shells, h. 14″
Lent by Mr. and Mrs. John Bertalan

Paired, joined male and female dance images for Eshu are worn hanging upside down around the neck. Cowrie shells, formerly the major currency in Yorubaland, hang from the bases of the figures. Cowries honor Eshu, but money can also bring trouble. Acknowledging this, altars to Eshu are found at crossroads and marketplaces, locations of potential conflict. Both figures have knives springing from their heads, a symbol of wonder-working powers and sensuality.

Thompson, 1971, CH 4/1-3.

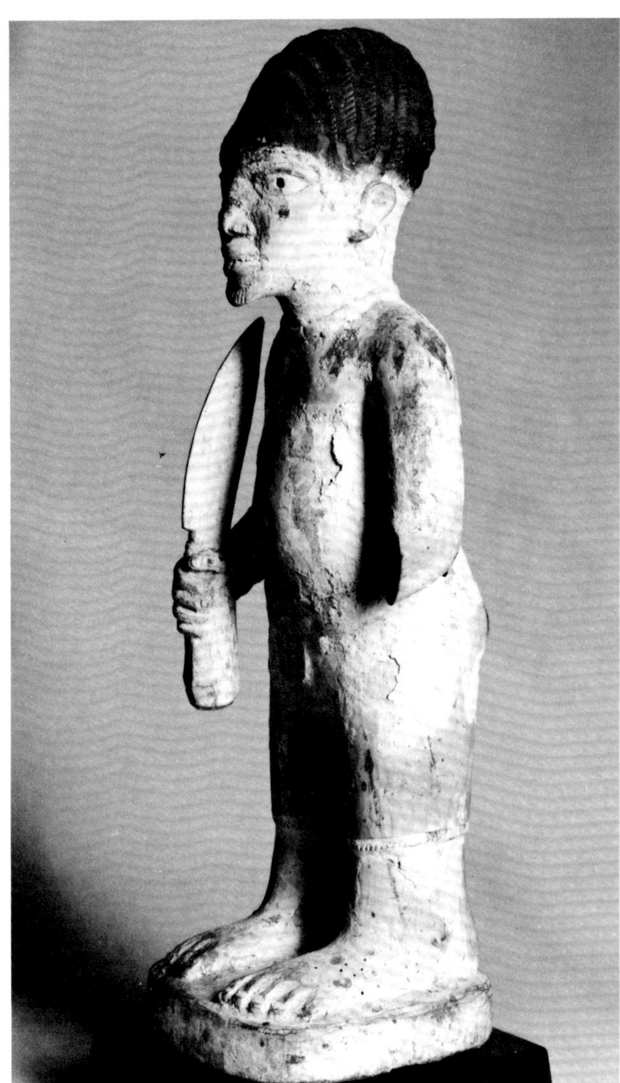

27. OGUN SHRINE SCULPTURE
Yoruba, Awori, Ota
Wood, pigment, h. 19″
Private collection

Ogun, the Yoruba orisha of iron, is worshipped by those who use or have a special relationship with this metal. These include blacksmiths, warriors, hunters and, today, drivers of motorized vehicles. Figurative sculpture related to the worship of Ogun is uncommon. The rigid posture and intense stare of this figure may denote one in a state of possession by the deity.

Fagg and Pemberton, 1982. ill. pl. 52 p. 157.

28. STAFF FOR OGUN (*IWANA OLOGUN*)
Yoruba
Brass and iron, h. 28½″
Seattle Art Museum, Katherine White Collection

Iron staffs with brass heads serve as title staffs for the chief of blacksmiths and emblems of war chiefs. These staffs are in the form of pokers which blacksmiths use to rake ashes.

Thompson, 1974. ill. pl. 95, p. 71.
Thompson, 1971. CH 7/1-2.

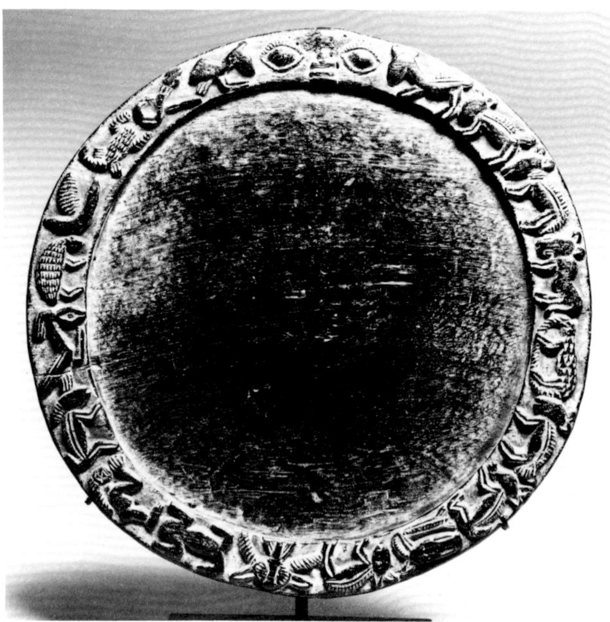

29. IFA DIVINATION TRAY (*OPON IFA*)
Yoruba, Erin-Ilobu-Oshogbo sector
Wood, h. 14½″
Private collection

Divination is the process by which humans can communicate with the gods. This contact helps them to understand the direction of their lives and the meaning and significance of events. The priest of Ifa, the orisha of divination, acts as an intermediary in this process. Through the manipulation of palm nuts, a divining chain or cowrie shells, he determines the number of marks to make on a wood dust covered tray such as this one. Different combinations of marks call for the recitation of certain verses of the Ifa oral literature (*odu Ifa*). A diviner must study for many years to master this extensive oral literature. The myths, poetry and history he recites enlighten the supplicant and suggest solutions to problems or an appropriate course of action.

Orunmila or Ifa, the orisha of fate is paired in Yoruba thought with Eshu, the orisha of chance. A primary element on all opon Ifa is the face of Eshu. When the divination tray is in use, the face of Eshu is placed opposite the diviner. In this example, Eshu appears a second time in profile wearing his characteristic long-tailed hairdo. Numerous animal representations complete the motifs on this piece.

Fagg and Pemberton, 1982. ill. pl. 60. p. 173.

30. DIVINATION TAPPER (*IROKE IFA*)
Yoruba, Oyo area
Ivory, h. 11″
Private collection

The *babalawo* (priest of Ifa), taps an iroke Ifa against his divination tray to invoke the gods at the start of a divining session. A kneeling woman is often depicted on an iroke Ifa. Her posture indicates submission to a greater authority while her breast-holding gesture symbolizes generosity and acceptance of her female role as nurturer.

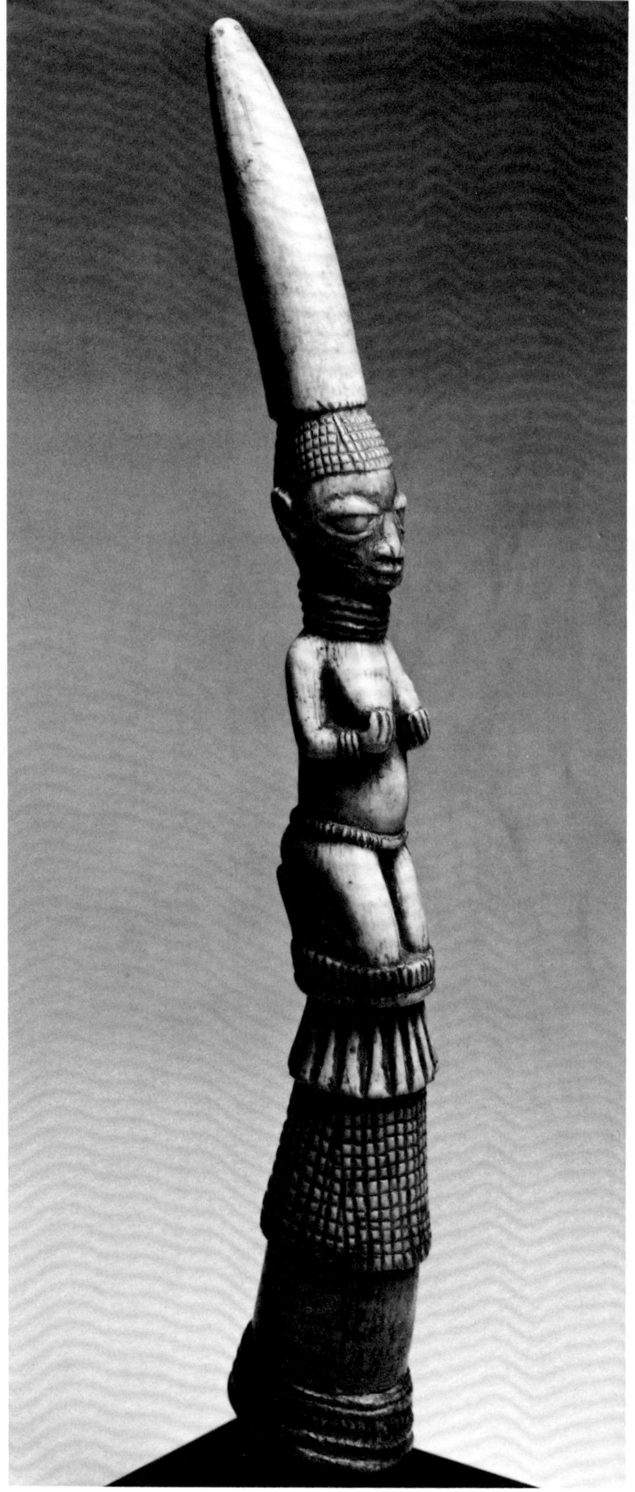

30

Fagg and Pemberton, 1982. ill. pl. 35. p. 123.
Thompson, 1974. p. 54.

31. DIVINATION TAPPER (*IROKE IFA*)
Yoruba
Wood, h. 13″
Lent by Dr. Mike Callahan

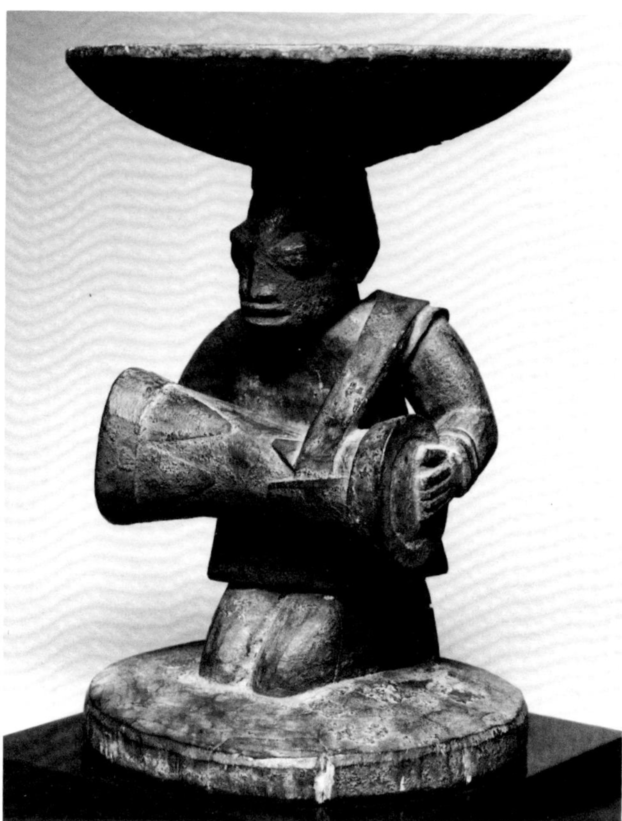

32. DIVINATION CUP (*AGERE IFA*)
Yoruba
Wood, h. 8¾″
Lent by Edward M. Friend III

Cups to hold the sixteen sacred palm nuts used in divination are carved with a great variety of subject matter. This agere Ifa depicts a kneeling drummer playing a *bata* drum, a type of instrument associated with Shango, the thunder god, in western Yorubaland.

Fagg and Pemberton, 1982. p. 54.

33. DIVINATION CUP (*AGERE IFA*)
Yoruba
Wood, pigment, h. 7″
Lent by Dr. John Nixon

This polychrome divination cup has as its motif a mounted horseman and two standing figures. They hold staffs and guns which support the edges of the cup in which the sacred palm nuts for Ifa divination are placed.

34. DIVINATION CUP (*AGERE IFA*)
Yoruba
Wood, h. 8¼″
Lent by Mrs. Katherine Phillips Jacobs

The interlocking abstract design is reminiscent of the continuous interlace pattern known as *ebo* which appears on garments and other objects associated with kingship. It is said to suggest the difficulty in resolving the intricate problems of life and matters of state.

Thompson, 1976. p. 18/3.

35. DIVINATION CUP (*AGERE IFA*)
Yoruba
Wood, h. 9½″
Lent by Odessa Woolfolk

36. DIVINER'S BAG (*APO IFA*)
Yoruba
Glass beads, cloth, wood, h. 12½″
Lent by Pace Gallery

Solidly beaded garments and accessories are usually reserved for use by Yoruba royalty and priests of certain orisha. They may be worn by priests of Ifa, the "king" of Yoruba cults. A diviner stores objects used in the divination rites in bags such as this one. Birds which appear in relief are found frequently in objects associated with Ifa and refer to the healing arts of herbalism as well as to the spiritual powers of the mothers. Cowrie shells which here serve as a strap are sometimes used in divination.

Fagg, 1980. p. 16.

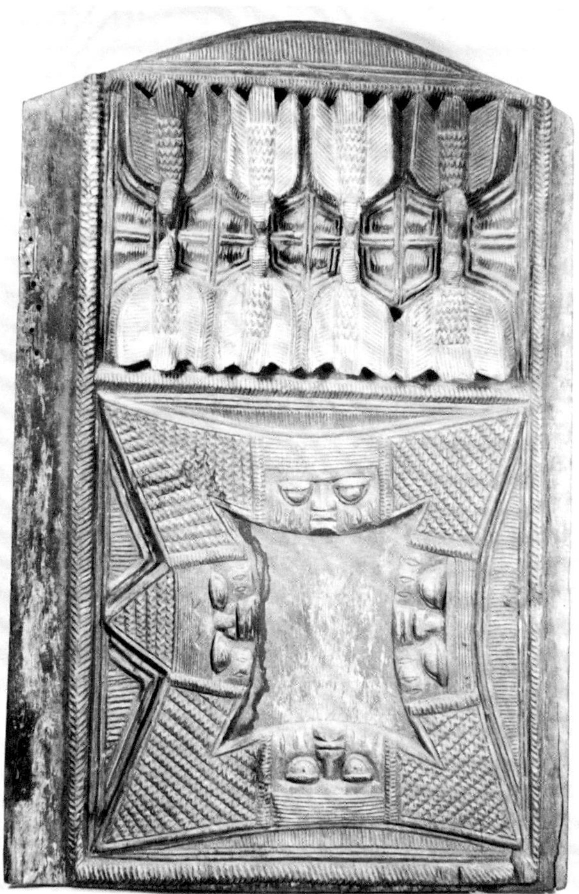

37. DECORATIVE ARCHITECTURAL PANEL OR DOOR
Yoruba
Wood, pigment, h. 40″
National Museum of African Art

Carved doors and panels adorn houses of the wealthy and religious shrines. This panel shows a divination board with four heads of Eshu, the trickster orisha and two rows of four birds each. It may have covered a window in the house of a diviner.

Blue, associated with coolness, is a color preferred by the Yoruba.

Thompson, 1971.

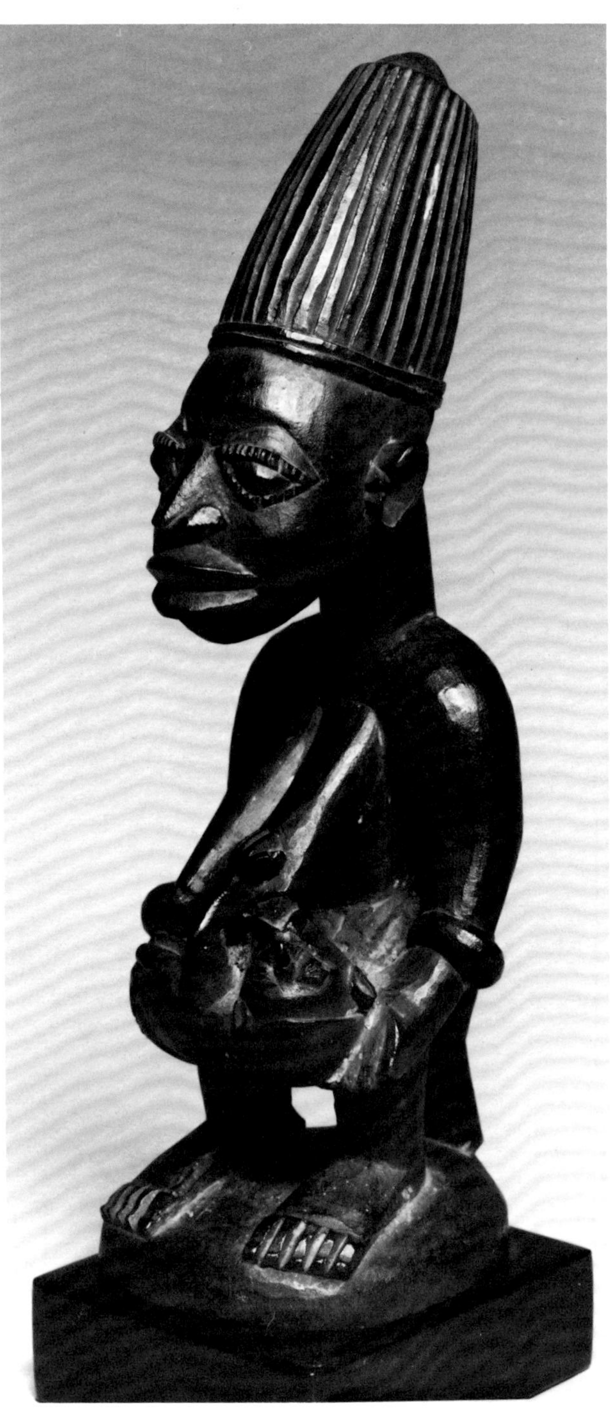

38. MATERNITY FIGURE
Yoruba, Oshugbo
Wood, h.12″
Mr. and Mrs. Louis J. Willie

Carved representations of mothers and children are placed in shrines for many Yoruba orisha as symbols of the fertility granting powers of these deities or as gifts of thanksgiving for the birth of a child.

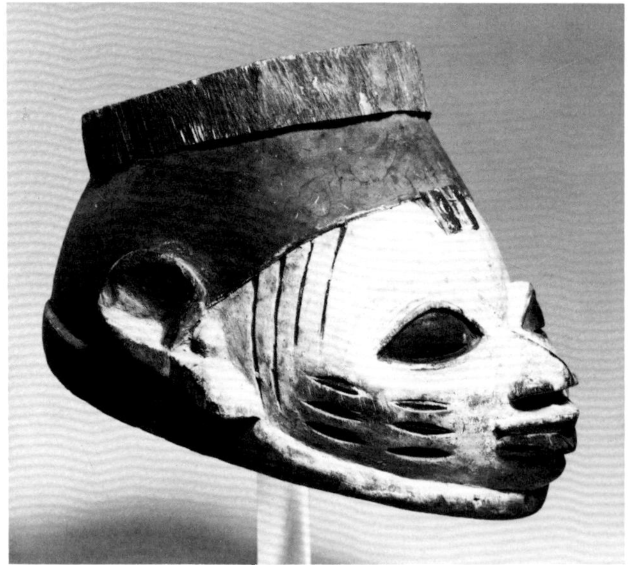

39. HEADDRESS FOR *GELEDE* MASQUERADE
Yoruba, Ketu
Wood, pigment, h.8″
Birmingham Museum of Art, gift of Dr. Richard G. Hammett in memory of his grandfather, Walter Engel Grindstaff 1983.52

The masked festivals known as *Gelede* are performed in western Yorubaland to honor the special powers of women (see photograph I). Elderly women, female deities and female ancestors are thought to possess great power (*ashe*). This power is morally neutral and can have destructive as well as positive effects on the community. Masked Gelede performers who are male attempt to cajole and flatter these women known as "the mothers" so that their force can be directed toward beneficial purposes.

Gelede masks consist of a rounded head portion with a symmetrical, calm face. In many examples, this is topped by a superstructure that can be quite elaborate. It often contains complex figure or animal compositions which illustrate and comment upon many aspects of Yoruba life. The superstructure has been removed from this example. Masks are painted, and white, the color associated with the "cool" orisha and post menopausal women, is frequently used. White connotes purity, calmness and patience, soothing feminine qualities. Gelede masks are worn on top of the head, and the face of the dancer is concealed by a cloth covering. Costuming for dancers who represent women emphasizes the female figure and can have false breasts and exaggerated buttocks. Maskers representing male characters wear brightly colored panels that emphasize the bulk of the body. Dancing styles differ as well.

This mask closely resembles an example attributed by Drewal and Drewal to the Etuobe workshop. The Ketu Yoruba live on both sides of the Nigeria/Republic of Benin (Dahomey) border and primarily reside in Benin.

H. Drewal, 1974. pp. 8-11.
Drewal and Drewal, 1983. pp. 81, 168, 287, pl. 90.

40. HEADDRESS FOR *GELEDE* MASQUERADE
Yoruba, Egbado
Wood, h.11½″
Private collection

This female Gelede dance headdress has a swirling head tie which crosses in the back. In performance, the interwoven forms echo the elaborate curving motions of the dancers' arms and bodies. Traditionally, Gelede maskers perform in matched pairs providing another level of visual complexity.

Drewal and Drewal, 1983.

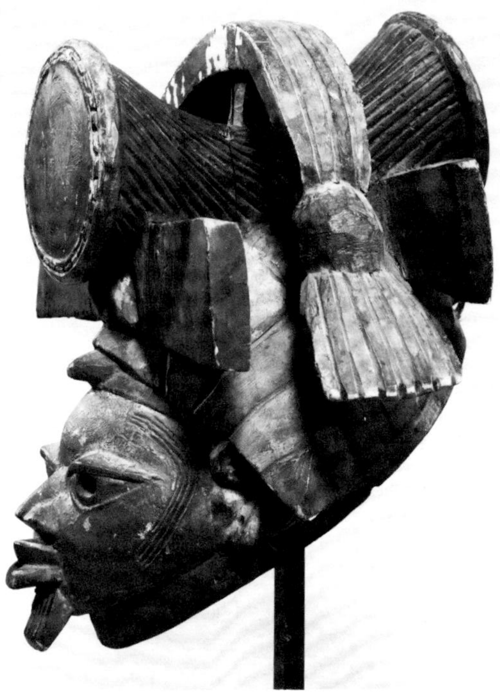

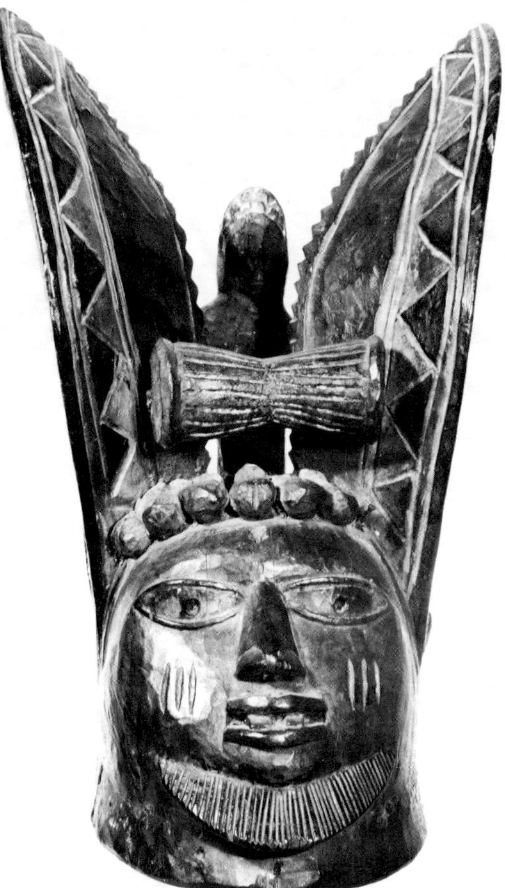

41. HEADDRESS FOR *GELEDE* MASQUERADE
Yoruba. Oyo
Wood, pigment h. 10½″
Lent by Kathleen Nelson and Robert Goldenberg

This Gelede mask of the male type has an elaborate superstructure which includes a *dundun* (pressure drum), striped cap and cloth tie. The beard may indicate that this mask represents a Muslim.

The paired Gelede dancers that appear in the afternoon performance represent all aspects of Yoruba life: various age groups, social, economic, political and religious roles. Masks are worn which employ humor and satire to ridicule antisocial elements. Other masks may relate to concepts about forces of the cosmos.

Drewal and Drewal, 1983. pp. 162.

42. *EFE/GELEDE* NIGHT HEADDRESS (*APASA*)
Yoruba. Ohori
Wood, pigment h. 18″
Lent by William Arnett

During *Efe*, the night performance preceding the daytime Gelede masquerade, a variety of mask types, both male and female, are used. Among the Ohori Yoruba, performers wearing male masks known as *apasa* sing during Efe ceremonies. They have carved, fan-like beards and vertical projections at either side of the face which are called either ears or cutlasses. Masks present a vision of male physical and spiritual power. Maskers are clothed in palm fronds, one of many references to Ogun (see cat nos. 27, 28) in this masquerade.

H. Drewal, 1980. ill. p. 74. cat no. 130.
Drewal and Drewal, 1983. pp. 85-96. ill. p. 96, pl. 39.

43. HEADDRESS (*EGUNGUN ERIN*)
Yoruba, Egbado, Abeokuta
Wood, paint h. 13½″
Lent by Michael A. Gold

Among the Yoruba, the dead are believed to influence the fortunes of their descendants. *Egungun* masquerades exist among all Yoruba subgroups and honor the spirits of the ancestors. It is in this form that the dead are believed to return in physical form to interact with their descendants and to reinforce their bond with the living.

The word *egungun* in its broadest sense refers to any masquerade or masked figure. *Egungun* as a concept varies greatly among Yoruba subgroups. In some cases, the masquerade is said to represent ancestors or to partake of their spiritual power, and, in others, it is said to represent orisha.

Egungun masquerades can also serve as status symbols for the living. This type of headdress is called *egungun erin* (elephant). The term refers not only to the size and large ears of the carving but also to the owner's wealth and pride in his lineage. Power references include the small carved gourds across the forehead representing containers of potency-enhancing medicines, the drum and the animal carved on the back.

Egungun costumes are usually composed of many layers of cloth. They take many forms and may or may not include a carved wooden headdress. The erin headdress is worn with an elaborate, colorful costume made of expensive materials. Both the materials and the iconography of the erin costume refer to traditional Yoruba royalty.

Wolf, in Vogel, ed., 198 1 pp. 110-111.
H. Drewal, 1978. p. 18.
Lawal, 1977. pp. 57-59.

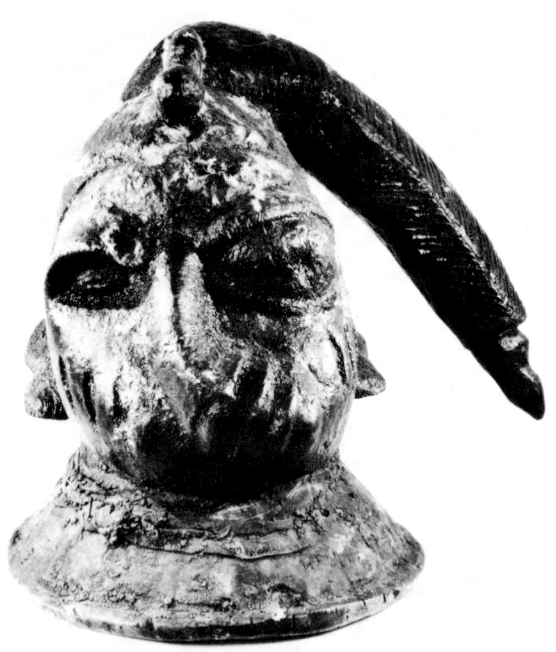

44. EGUNGUN HEADDRESS
Yoruba
Wood, h. 14"
L. Kahan Gallery

The Yoruba sometimes produce carvings which exaggerate, distort or reverse their usual canons of artistic expression for reasons of satire or social commentary. The twisted nose and mouth indicate a diseased person and social outcast.

Blier, 1982. p. 70, ill. fig 40 p. 48.

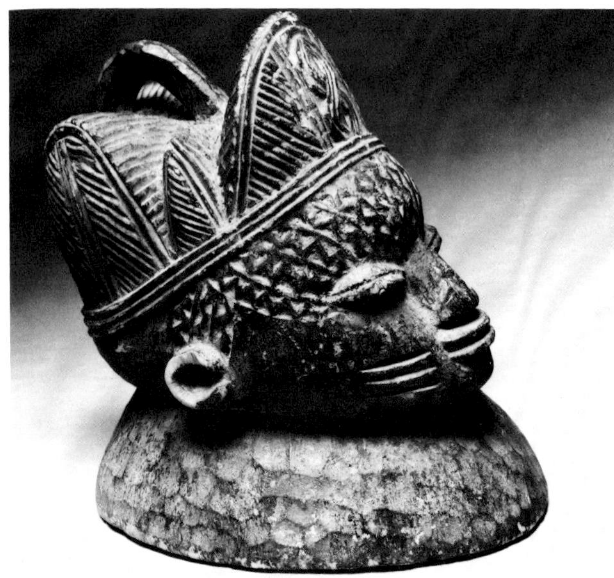

45. EGUNGUN HEADDRESS
Yoruba
Wood, h. 12"
Lent by Dr. and Mrs. Clifton Latting

The crown-like hat or hair treatment of this headdress with heavy surface patterning is decorated with the interlock design called ebo. (see cat no. 34)

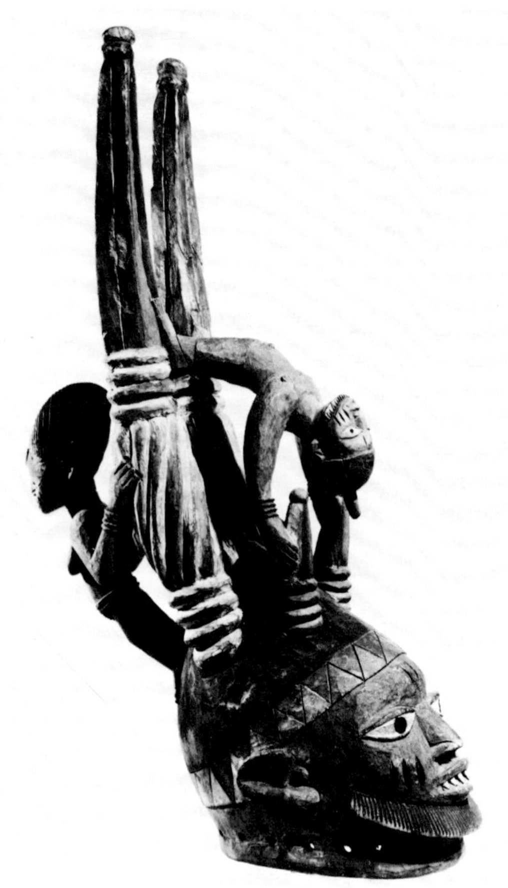

46. *ORO* HEADDRESS
Yoruba, Egbado/Egba, Abeokuta
Wood, pigment h. 32¼"
Lent by William Arnett

The *Oro* is a secret society which carries out judgments handed down by the Ogboni society (see cat no. 8). In the past, the Oro cult was responsible for the secret execution of witches. A cult official wears a mask of this type with a costume of palm fronds.

Henry Drewal attributes this mask to Oganbayo Akiode of the Esubiyi school and dates it to the 1940s.

H. Drewal, 1980. p. 87. ill. cat no. 154.

47. HEADDRESS FOR *EPA* MASQUERADE
Yoruba, Ekiti, Osi-Ilorin area
Wood, pigment, h. 50"
Lent by Pace Gallery

The *Epa* festival is held only in the northeastern part of Yoruba territory. Enormous masks which can weigh up to sixty pounds are worn to memorialize ancestral culture heroes and are owned by particular lineage groups. Masks are the focus of offerings and praise, and their athletic young wearers affirm the physical strength and achievements of the living. In some areas the wearer of a type of Epa mask must jump onto a mound of dirt and maintain his balance. His success is considered a good omen for the community.

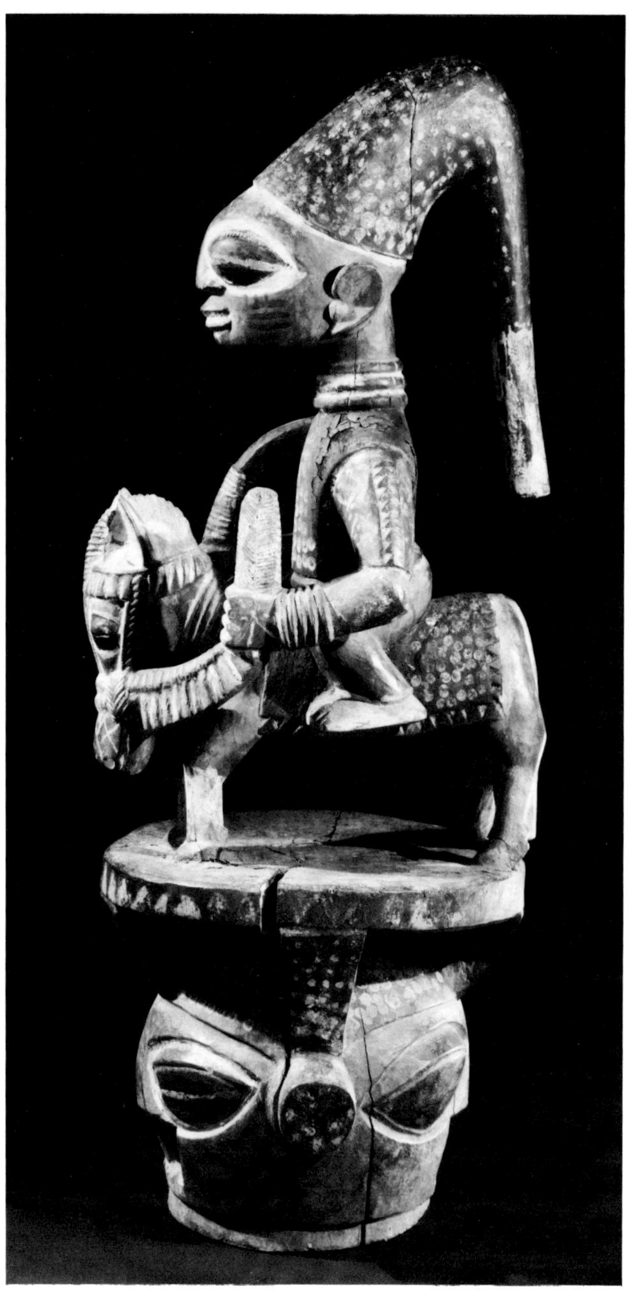

47

Epa masks consist of a janus pot-shaped helmet topped by a complex superstructure of one or more figures. The figurative superstructure depicts certain idealized types: the mother, the herbalist, the king or, as in this example, the equestrian hunter. The abstracted mask combines with the more naturalistic figure and fuses elements of spiritual and ancestral power. Masks are repainted before use and are worn with a body covering of palm fronds.

Fagg and Pemberton, pp. 132-133, 200, ill. pl. 40, p. 133.
Thompson, 1974. pp. 191-198.

48. FRAGMENT OF AN IVORY SWORD (*UDOMALORE*)

Yoruba, Owo
Ivory, h. 8⅝″
Late nineteenth century
The Paul and Ruth Tishman Collection

The Yoruba kingdom of Owo located in the eastern part of Yorubaland has a complex artistic heritage. Strong Edo influences are present in art and customs deriving from a geographic proximity to Edo peoples and periods of control by the Edo kingdom of Benin.

Ornate costumes worn by high ranking chiefs are said to have been introduced from the court of Benin in the seventeenth century. The most important chiefs were granted the right to wear an intricately carved or cast decorative sword (*udamalore*). This fragment was probably part of an udamalore and shows a figure holding a sword in his right hand and wearing another sword at his waist.

Poynor in Vogel, ed., 1981. pp. 133-134. ill. pl. 76, p. 133.
Sieber and Ruben, 1968. ill. no. 83.
Poynor, 1976. pp. 40-42.

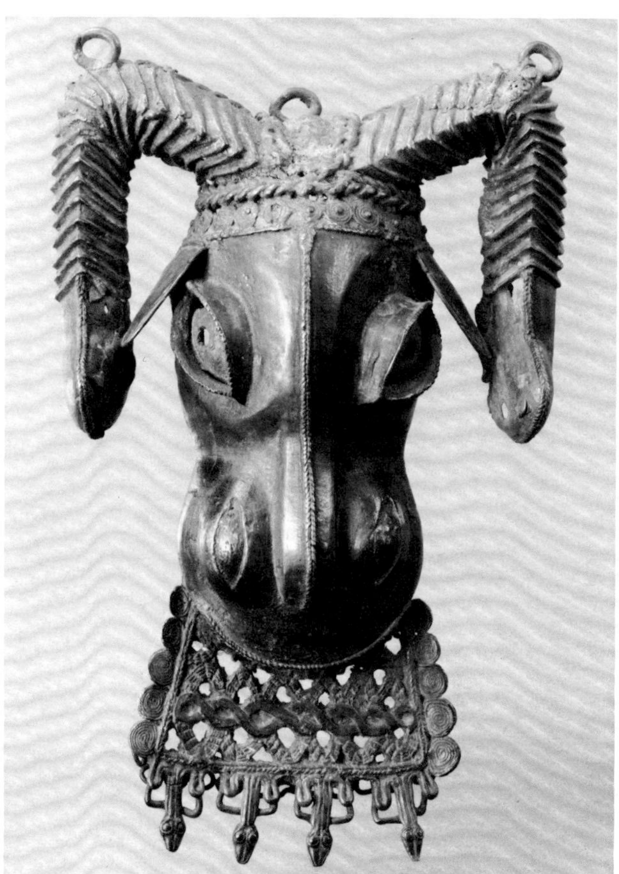

49. RAM'S HEAD MASK

Yoruba. Owo
Brass. h. 11″
Seattle Art Museum, Katherine White Collection, 81.17.495

In Owo, the depiction of rams refers to ancestral powers. This ram's head mask was part of a group of small brass or ivory sculptures attached to the *orufonran* costume worn by high-ranking chiefs (see photograph G). Adornments and costumes are of Benin derivation. A number of Yoruba, Edo, Igala and Igbo groups who were once subservient to the Benin kingdom use such masks as ritual paraphernalia. Masks come in ram, leopard and human versions.

Robin Poynor, personal communication, 1984.
Roache, 1972. ill. cat no. 8, p. 66.

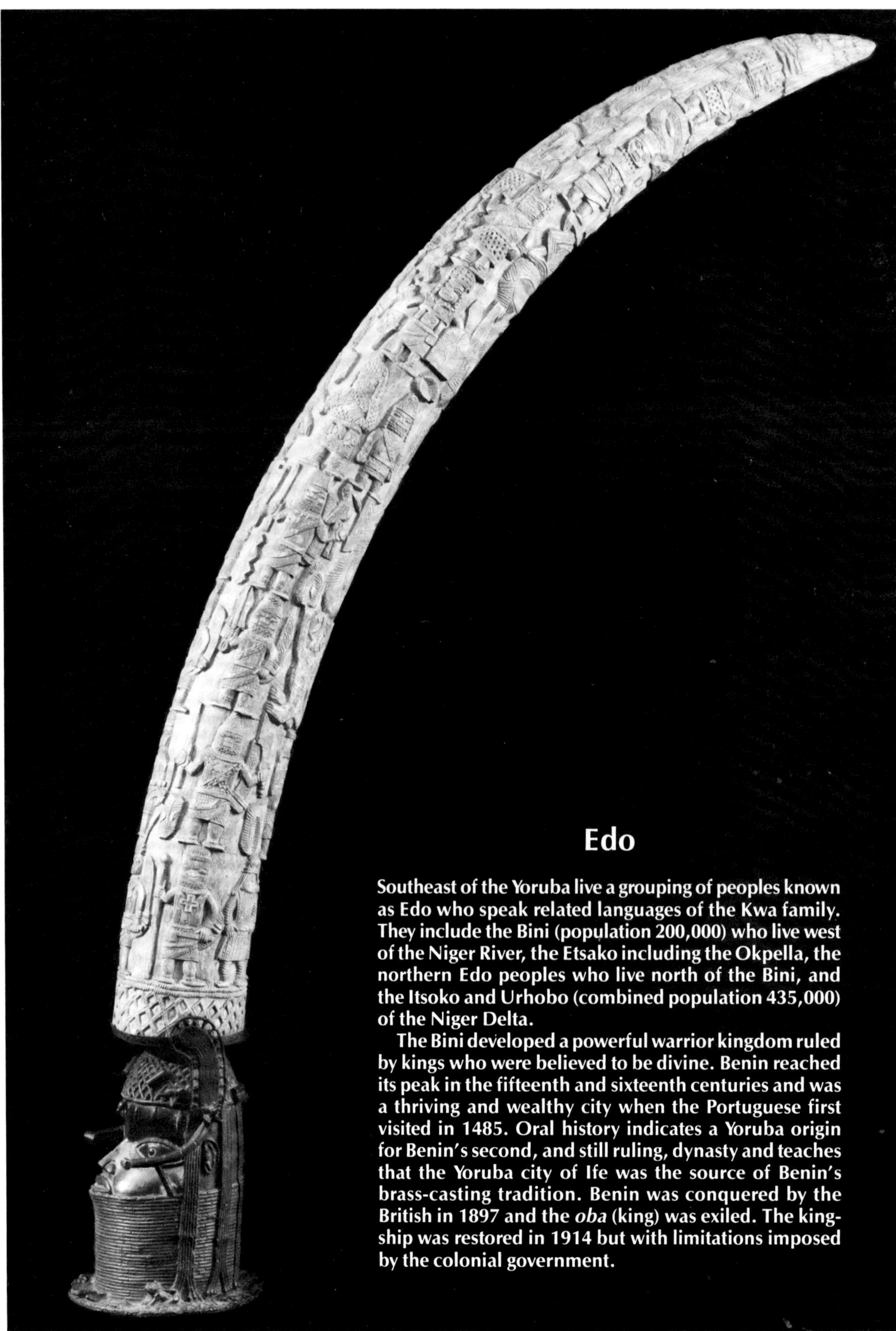

Edo

Southeast of the Yoruba live a grouping of peoples known as Edo who speak related languages of the Kwa family. They include the Bini (population 200,000) who live west of the Niger River, the Etsako including the Okpella, the northern Edo peoples who live north of the Bini, and the Itsoko and Urhobo (combined population 435,000) of the Niger Delta.

The Bini developed a powerful warrior kingdom ruled by kings who were believed to be divine. Benin reached its peak in the fifteenth and sixteenth centuries and was a thriving and wealthy city when the Portuguese first visited in 1485. Oral history indicates a Yoruba origin for Benin's second, and still ruling, dynasty and teaches that the Yoruba city of Ife was the source of Benin's brass-casting tradition. Benin was conquered by the British in 1897 and the *oba* (king) was exiled. The kingship was restored in 1914 but with limitations imposed by the colonial government.

50, 51

50, 51. COMMEMORATIVE HEAD (*UHUMWELAO*) AND CARVED TUSK

Benin court style
Brass, ivory, h. 14½", 63¾"
head, nineteenth century
The Milton D. Ratner Family Collection

In Benin, ancestral altars are established by the senior son as a focus for offerings to and communication with a deceased man. Altars to commoners and chiefs contain wooden objects, but royal altars contain sculpture made of the precious and highly symbolic materials, brass and ivory. While ancestral heads of commoners refer specifically to their own lineage, royal heads embody the welfare, prosperity and survival of the people as a whole. Brass symbolizes the permanence and continuity of the kingship and has both beauty and the power to drive away evil. Ivory is costly, charged with spiritual force and symbolic of strength, aggression, longevity and kingship.

A royal ancestral memorial is in the form of a stylized representation of the head of the deceased ruler wearing a profusion of coral beads, part of the royal costume. An elephant tusk carved with historical and symbolic representations protrudes from the top. A group of heads along with other memorial materials is placed on a clay altar in the palace and is the object of veneration and the locus of cyclical rituals and sacrifices.

This head dates from the nineteenth century, as the projecting winged decorations are considered to have been innovations during the reign of Oba Osemwede (1814-48). The protruding bead ornament is called "you can never touch the leopard's forehead"; the king was called "the leopard of the house." The tusk is probably of an earlier date.

H. Drewal, 1977. p. 30-35, ill. pl. 30 a, b, c.
Ben-Amos, 1980. pp. 57-68.
Blackmun in Ben Amos and Rubin, ed., 1983. pp. 59-60.
Dark in McCall and Bay, ed., 1975. p. 42.

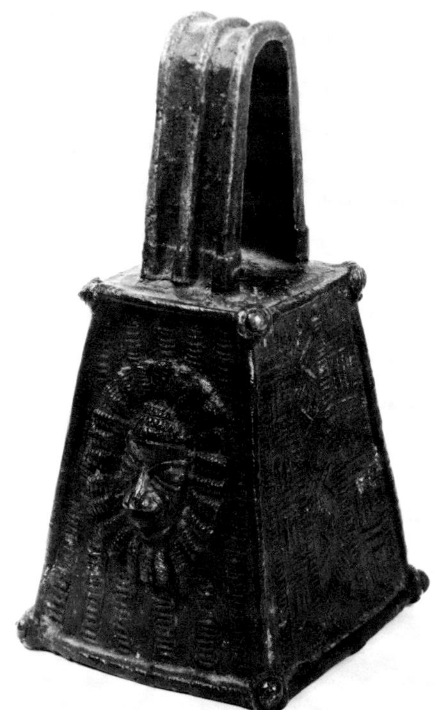

52

52. PYRAMIDAL BELL (*ERORO*)

Benin court style
Brass, h. 6½"
Nineteenth century
Lent by Tony Harrison and Pat Tyson

Pyramidal brass bells were important in the religious and political life of the Benin kingdom. They were worn, sometimes on a leopard-tooth collar, around the necks of chiefs and retainers as a sign of military rank. These bells were also placed on ancestral altars and used to summon spirits or announce the beginning of a religious festival.

A Catalog of a Collection of Benin Works of Art, 1980. ill. no. 3, p. 13.
Hess in Ben Amos and Rubin, ed., 1983. pp. 103-106.

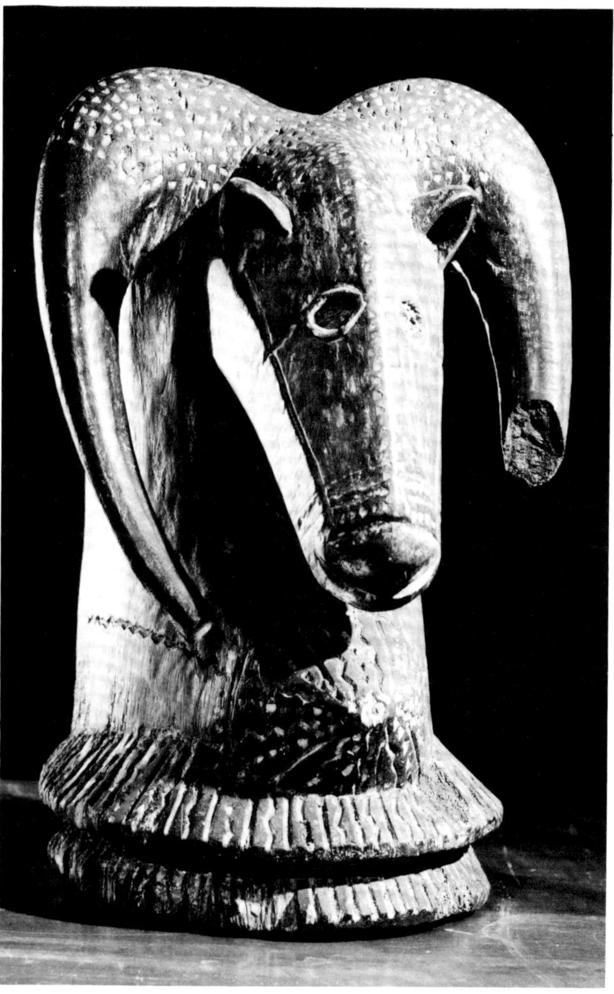

53. COMMEMORATIVE HEAD (*UHUMWELAO*)

Northern Edo
Wood, h. 14¾"
Field Museum of Natural History, Chicago

Wooden rams' heads are placed on ancestral altars of chiefs of royal lineage by the Yoruba of Owo as well as by chiefs of the Bini and related Edo groups. Sacrifices are made before them at the time of the cutting of the first yams of the year. Fagg attributes this ram's head to the Bini from an outlying part of Benin territory or to the Edo-speaking Ishan (see photograph F).

Fagg, 1963. ill. pl. 105.
Balandier and Maquet, 1974. ill. p. 138.

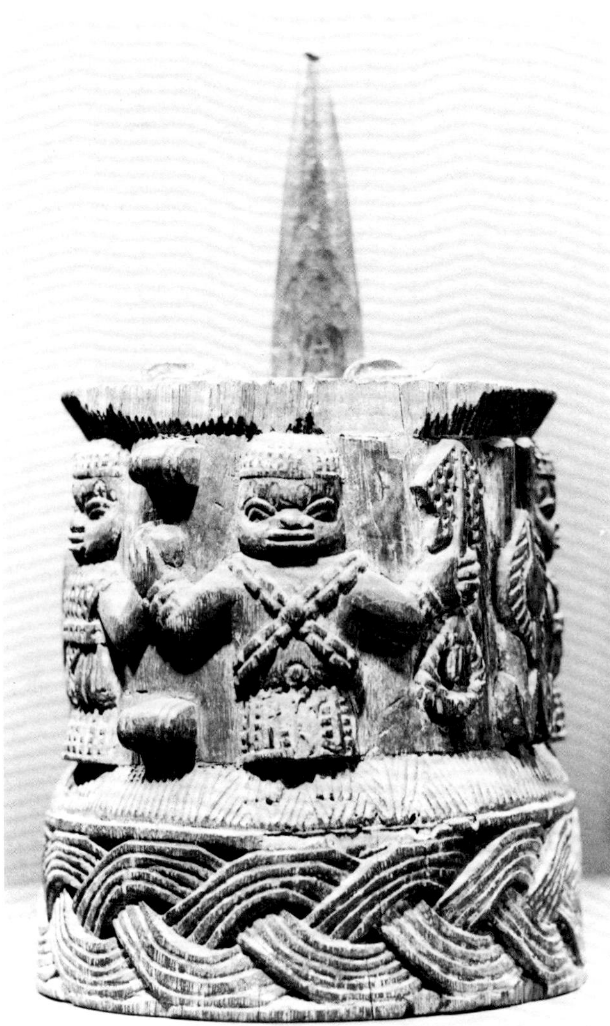

54. ALTAR OF THE HAND (*IKEGOBO*)
Bini

Wood, h. 14″
National Museum of African Art, gift of Harold Rome

While the head symbolizes thinking, judgment and character, the hand stands for individual success. Shrines to the hand are made by many peoples throughout southern Nigeria. The altar to the hand (*ikegobo*) in Benin may be made of wood or brass for royalty and certain war chiefs and consists of a cylindrical base with a projecting pointed peg to support a horn or tusk. A representation of the owner along with attendants and warriors appears in relief on the ikegobo.

Vogel, 1974. pp. 8-10, ill. pl 27, p. 10.
Dean, Schaefer in Ben Amos and Rubin, 1983. pp. 33-37, 71.

55. HEADPIECE AND COSTUME (*ODOGO*)
Northern Edo, Etsako

Lawrence Ajanaku of the Okpella people
Cloth appliqué
Lent by Museum of Cultural History, UCLA, gift of
Mrs. W. Thomas Davis in memory of W. Thomas Davis

Around 1920, the northern Edo people adopted a masquerade performance known as *Okakagbe*. The first appliqué costumes were made by an artist named Okeleke who came from the Igbo-Igala borderland. This tradition has continued, and today the major maker of appliqué costumes is Lawrence Ajanaku. This costume is part of a group that was commissioned by UCLA between 1972-1974.

Okakagbe is a daytime masquerade of great beauty that entertains the people during religious festivals. The ensemble consists of five or six anthropomorphic figures costumed in cloth appliqué and one figure in the guise of a bush monster. All are believed to be spirit-figures. This costume is called Odogo (Ancient Mother). It is the most elaborate of the group and has a broad brimmed hat topped with stuffed cloth figures or children.

Borgatti, 1979. pp. 4-7 ill. p. 23

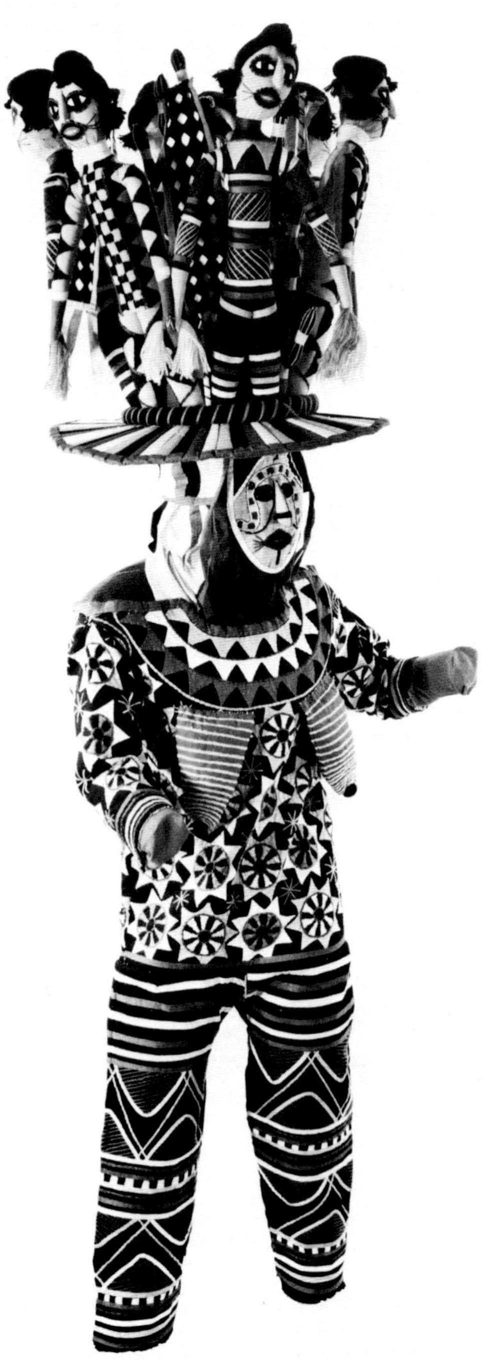

55

Niger Delta

The delta region of the Niger River is the home of the Ijo in the swampland to the south and the riverain Igbo, the Urhobo and the Isoko in the drier land to the north. The Ijo (population 175,000) are fishermen while the other peoples combine fishing with farming and harvesting palm fruit. Water spirits play an important role in indigeneous religious beliefs. Individual achievement is also celebrated in the personal shrine figures used in this region.

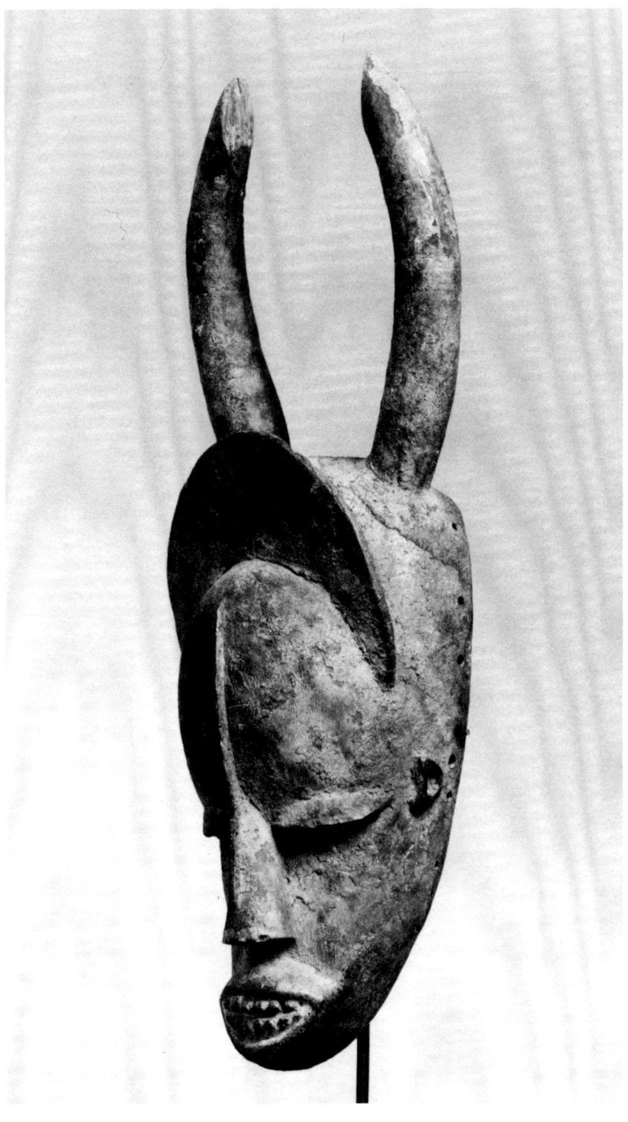

56. MASK FOR *OHWORU* MASQUERADE
Urhobo, southern
Wood, pigment, h. 19¼″
The Milton D. Ratner Family Collection

The *Ohworu* masquerade of the Urhobo people honors a powerful water spirit. Horns on masks may refer to animals of the bush or may be a reference to the traditional bridal coiffure worn by Urhobo women.

H. Drewal, 1977. p. 36, ill. pl. 33.

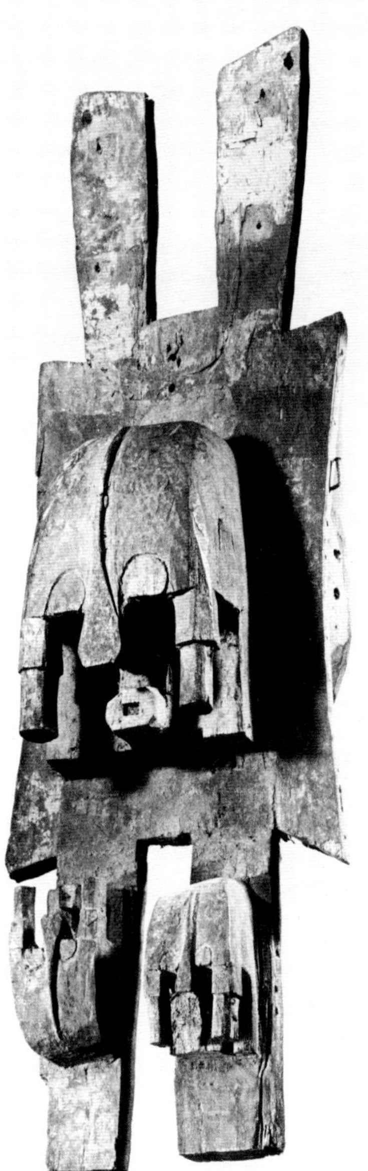

57. WATER SPIRIT HEADPIECE
Ijo
Wood, pigment, l. 33″
Lent by William Arnett

Many masquerades among the Ijo represent water spirits which live in every creek and control the environment. Masks are important not for their artistic significance but for securing the presence of the spirits, for it is through sculpture that men can control the spirits' powers. The most common position for wearing a mask is with the principle features facing the sky, and sometimes the sculpted wooden headdress is partially or totally obscured by other portions of the costume, emphasizing that the masks' primary audience is spiritual and not human. Masks often combine the features of water animals with those of humans.

The works of the Kalabari Ijo are the best known. This headpiece is from a non-Kalabari area and was probably worn for the *Ikulie* masquerade.

Horton, 1963. pp. 94-114.
Horton, 1965. pp. 4-12. cf. pl. 69.
Wittmer and Arnett, 1978 p. 38, ill. pl. 90.

58. FIGURE (*IVRI*)

Isoko, southern
Wood, h. 28″
Nineteenth-twentieth centuries
The Paul and Ruth Tishman Collection

Ivri figures of the Isoko vary widely in size and form. Beliefs of the Isoko relating to these objects show variation as well. The Isoko think of the quality, ivri, as adamance or forcefulness, a personality trait which is desired if not present in too great a quantity. Small personal ivri sculptures help control this trait while large ones serve a protective function for an entire clan. Ivri is also considered by some clans to be a protective deity.

Objects combining human and animal forms are used by the neighboring Urhobo and the Ijo for a similar purpose. Ivri also have certain iconographic similarities to the Bini and Igbo altars to the hand (cat nos. 54, 59, 60).

Peek in Vogel, ed., 1981. p. 140-143, ill. pl. 81.

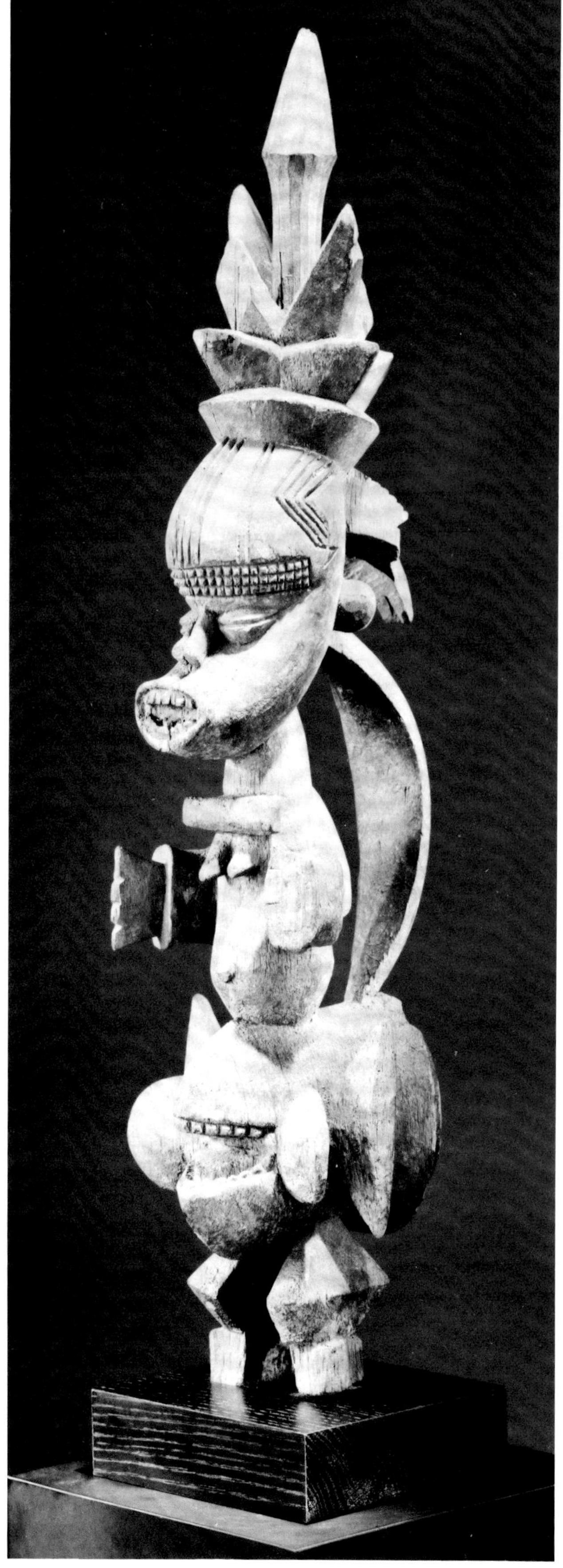

58

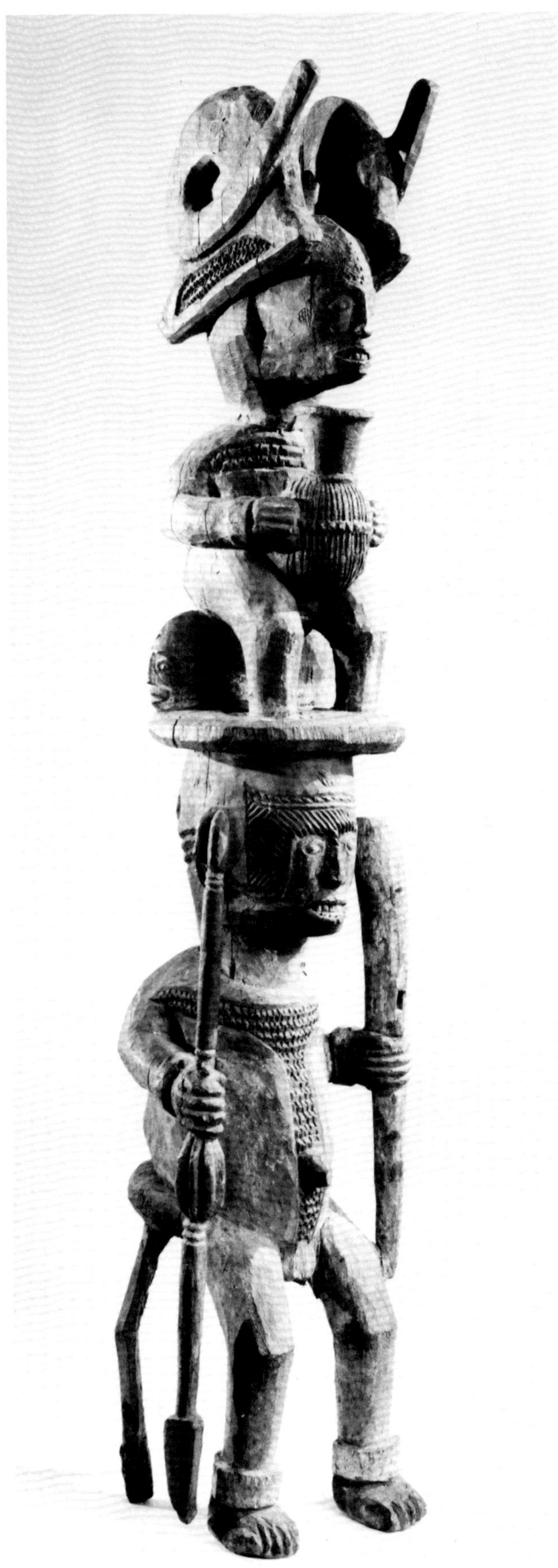

59

Igbo

Unlike the Yoruba and Bini, the Igbo (population 7,000,000), who are the second largest ethnic group in southern Nigeria, never formed centralized kingdoms or urban centers. Before the colonial period, the highest form of political authority rested at the village level. The majority of Igbo inhabit the forest and meadow region north of the Niger River Delta. It is this region of southeastern Nigeria which seceded in 1967 to form the Republic of Biafra and was reunited with the Federal Republic of Nigeria in 1970. There are over two hundred Igbo subgroups, and the linguistic and cultural variation among them is significant. Traditionally, men's societies played a large role in Igbo life, and masquerades were and, in some areas, still are performed by these groups. Artistic style varies widely from one part of Igbo territory to another reflecting their individualism and decentralized political structure.

59. PERSONAL SHRINE (*IKENGA*)

Igbo, Onitsha-Awka area
Wood, paint, h. 38¼″
Lent by Leonard and Judith Kahan

Ikenga of the Igbo of southern Nigeria are the best known of the male personal shrines made by many peoples of this region. They are associated with the owner's right hand and represent his strength, aggressiveness and powers of accomplishment. Some ikenga are minimal and may consist of a stool and horns, the required iconographic elements. Others, such as this one which was made for a title holder, can be quite elaborate. The seated owner wears forehead scarification, anklets and holds a horn and staff, all emblems of his titled status in a men's association. He supports a smaller horned figure seated on a severed head and holding a vessel. (see cat no. 69)

Vogel, 1974. p. 4, ill. no. 3
Mount, 1983, ill. cat no. 64.

60. PERSONAL SHRINE (*IKENGA*)

Igbo
Wood, sacrificial matter, h. 16½″
Private collection

This heavily incrusted ikenga shows evidence of its owner's sacrifices to it. The left hand holds a skull while the right, which has been removed, once held a machete. The ikenga wears the grass skirt of a warrior and the forehead scarification of a title holder. These combine with the typical attributes of horns and stool to project an image of aggression and high status.

Vogal, 1974. p .3.

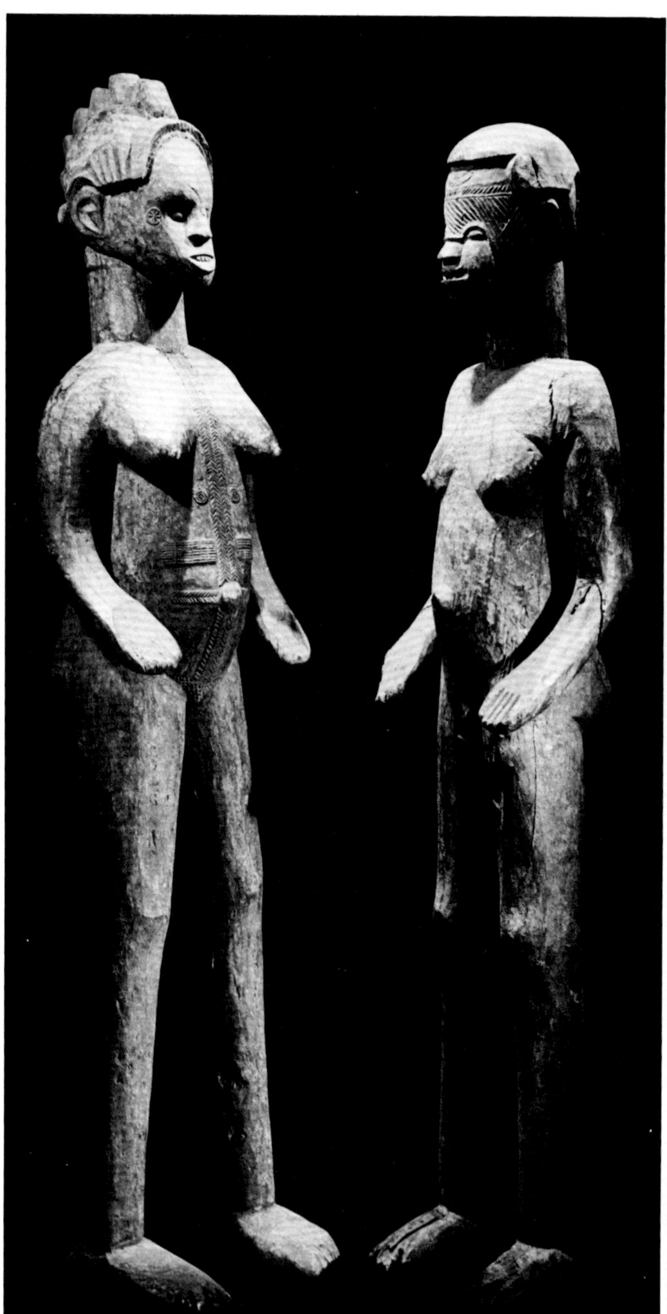

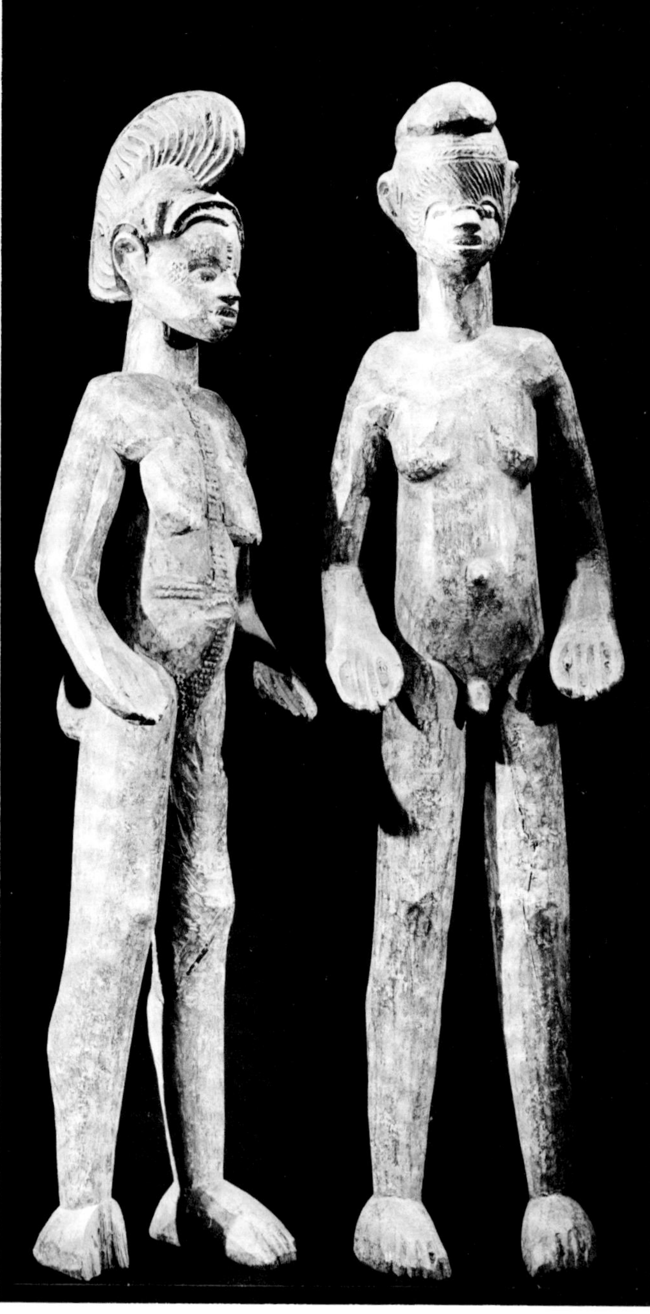

61.-64. SHRINE FIGURES
Igbo, Onitsha and Akwa Divisions
Wood, pigment h. 52", 49½, 46½", 47¼"
Lent by William Arnett

Among the Igbo of the north, wooden figures are carved to symbolize deities associated with the four days of the Igbo week and the local markets held on those days. They are housed in a decorated compound and are attended by priests who wash, polish, dress and present the figures on their special market day and annual ceremony of renewal. They receive offerings to honor and appease them. These gods are based on an idealized human model and show the attributes of wealth and power. Like humans, figures of market deities have possessions and family represented by other carvings. This grouping of figures is the work of a single carver and was probably from the same shrine.

Wittmer and Arnett, 1978, p. 15, cat no. 29-32.
Cole, 1969. pp. 39-41.

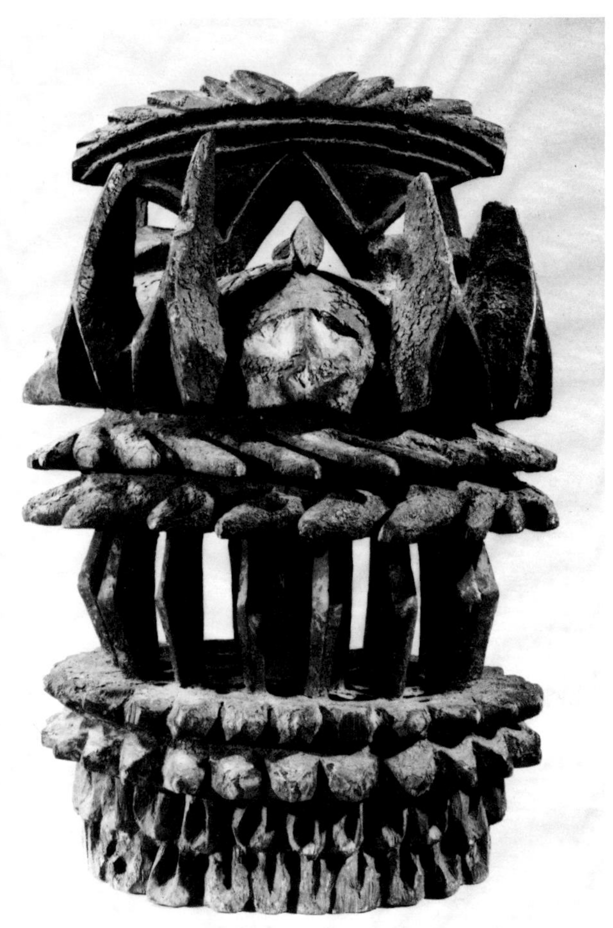

65. HEADPIECE
Igbo, Southwest, Okoba
Wood, h. 18½″
Lent by Leonard and Judith Kahan

A spiky, horned form reminiscent of a minimal ikenga is repeated around this cylindrical headpiece. This type of head covering is worn with a small, white *mmuo* mask covering the face. This combination of forms serves as another example of the concept of male/female duality presented in the form of a masquerade.

Mount, 1983. ill. cat no. 89.
H. Cole, quoted by L. Kahan, personal communication, 1983.

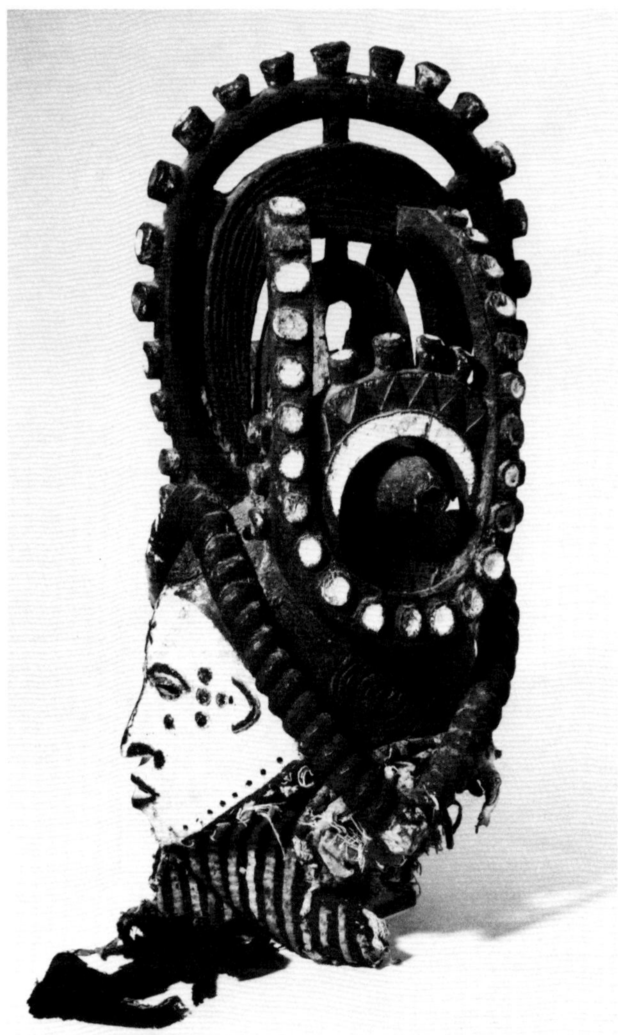

66. MAIDEN SPIRIT MASK (*AGBOGHO MMUO*)
Igbo
Wood, pigment, cloth h. 20″
Lent by Dr. and Mrs. Ralph Burton Pfeiffer Jr.

Masquerades on the theme of beauty and the beast are important among many southeastern Nigerian peoples. Beauty is represented by naturalistic masks with idealized human features while beast masks have a rough, grotesque and distorted appearance. Both types of masks are danced by men and may appear at the same performance, although at different times and with distinctly different dance styles. Masks are owned by men's societies which are traditionally associated with status in the community and perform important social control functions.

Members of the *Mmuo* association of the Igbo use white-faced spirit masks representing beautiful deceased maidens. They are danced at festivals at the beginning of the dry season and at funerals. White is associated with the ancestors as well as with wealth, beauty and goodness. The thin nose is believed to produce the high-pitched ancestral sound the dancers emit. Disk forms in the open braided hairdo suggest mirrors and a carved comb forms a central crest. Brightly colored fabric, part of the dancer's tight fitting costume, is still attached to this example. The intricate designs of the costume represent traditional female body decoration.

Blier, 1976.
Starkweather, 1966. p. 94.

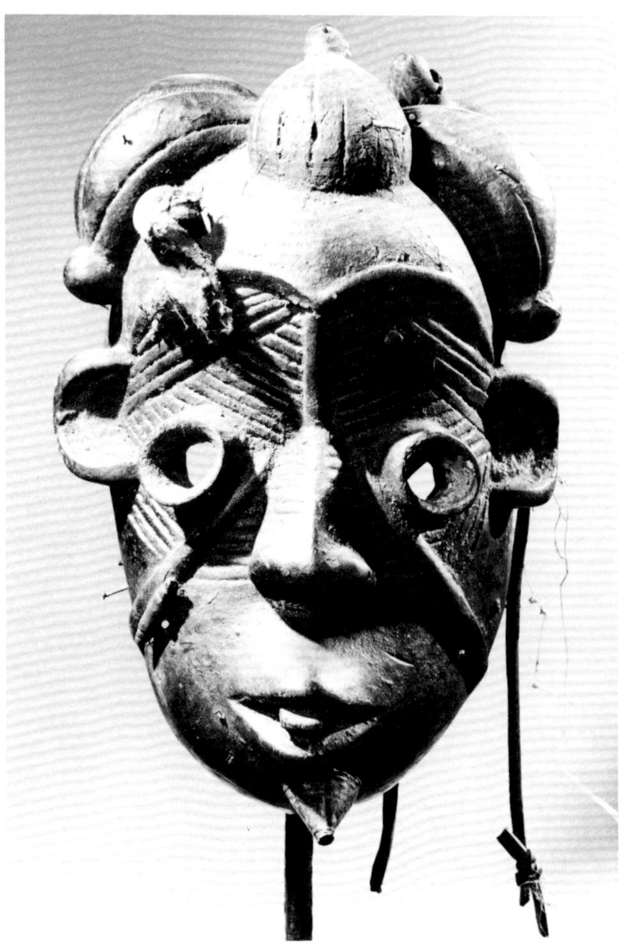

67. FACE MASK
Igbo, Onitsha region (?)
Wood, cloth, pigment, iron, h. 13″
The Milton D. Ratner Family Collection

Power enhancing additions in the form of carved calabash medicine containers and attached materials increase the potency of this beast-type mask. The dark color and protruding eyes are negative elements, and the protruding tongue connotes aggression.

Drewal, 1977. p. 44, ill. pl. 43.

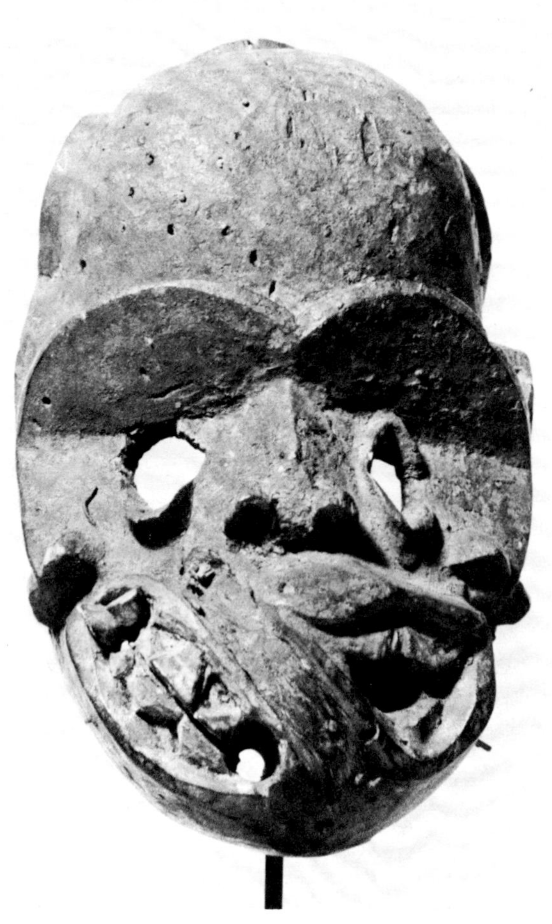

68. BEAST MASK (*OKOROSIA OJO*)
Igbo, Agwa
Wood, h. 12″
Lent by Leonard and Judith Kahan

In contrast to masks which represent beautiful spirits, beast masks are darkly colored and wear costumes of dirty rags or natural fibers, often with the addition of power-containing medicinal substances. This mask has two misshapen mouths as well as multiple noses and ears.

Herbert Cole has identified this mask as the work of the carver Anozie of the town of Agwa near Owerri. It was made for use in *Okorosia* plays which occur cyclically and honor the water spirit cult of the deity, Owu. There are forty or more characters in Okorosia, and each has an individual name, specific attributes of costuming and other equipment, music, songs and dance steps. The carved masks when seen alone belie the complexity of their content.

Blier, 1976. pp. 8-9.
H. Cole quoted by L. Kahan, personal communication, 1984.
Cole, 1969. pp. 36-38.
Mount, 1983. ill. cat no. 25.

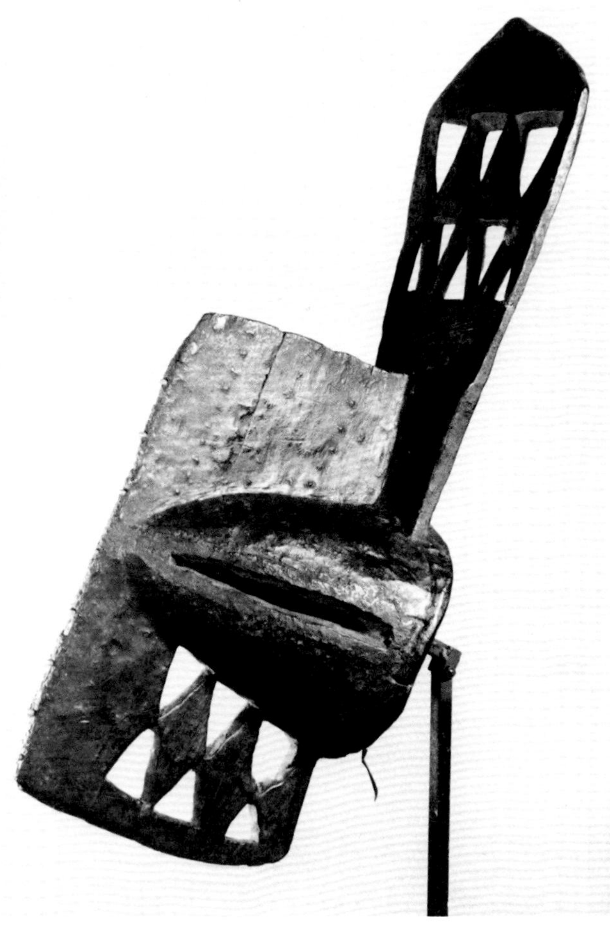

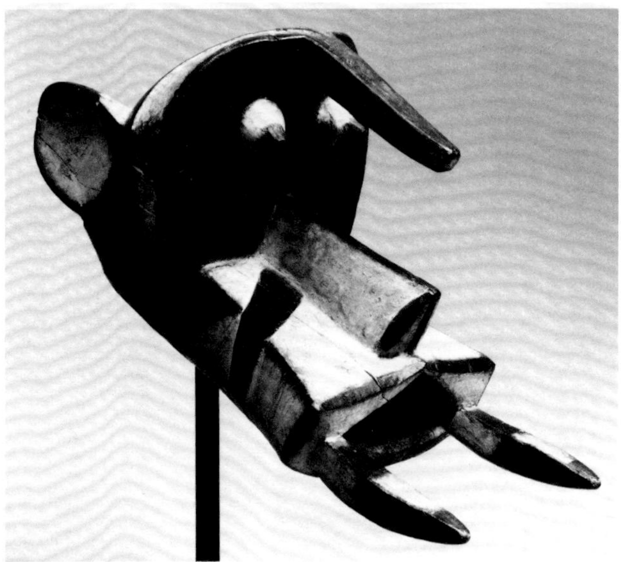

69. MASK
Igbo. Igbuka, Nzukka Division
Wood, h. 27 5/16″
Lent by Gene Willett

The use of geometric abstraction in this mask shows one of the various stylistic approaches found in Igbo sculpture. It was used during a title-taking ceremony.

The Igbo characteristics of individual competitiveness and desire for personal achievement are reflected in the importance of a system of title-taking. Through payment of ever increasing fees, a man can rise through the title hierarchy to positions of high status in the community. Titles carry with them the right to special names and the right to wear and display certain insignia. (see cat nos. 59 and 60)

Exhibitions to be Held on the Occasion of the First International Conference of African Culture. 1962. cf. cat no. 37.
Boston, 1977. pp. 10-13.

70. HORIZONTAL HEADDRESS (*OGBODO ENYI*)
Igbo, northeastern area
Wood, pigment l. 17″
Lent by J. T. Stephens

Animal masks in an elephant-human composite form are used by the northeastern Igbo of the Izi, Ezza and Ikwo subgroups. They are worn horizontally with a crocheted raffia costume with raffia ruffs at the neck and hem. Sometimes this type of mask combines a geometricized animal head facing forward with a more naturalistic representation of a human face facing backward. Masks such as this represent masculine aggressive forces. They are used as a part of the New Yam ceremonies and, more rarely, at chiefs' funerals.

Adams, 1982. p. 74-75.
Nyet, 1978. pp. 29-42.
Nyet, 1980.

72. FACE MASK (*ACALI*)

Igbo, Afikpo subgroup
Wood, pigment h. 11¼″
Lent by William Arnett

The *acali* is the first secret society mask that a young initiate wears. Although uncommon, it has several uses and is usually worn by the smallest boy taking part in the Okumkpa.

Wittmer and Arnett, 1978. p. 32, ill. cat no. 74.
Ottenberg, 1975. pp. 16-20.

73. FACE MASK (*MBA*)

Igbo, Afikpo subgroup
Wood, pigment h. 15¼″
Lent by William Arnett

The *mba* is a common mask worn by boys and young men who are dancers in the Okumkpa play. This white-faced mask is topped by a flat board covered with geometric or curvilinear designs.

Wittmer and Arnett, 1978. p. 33, ill. cat no. 75.
Ottenberg, 1974. pp. 27-31.

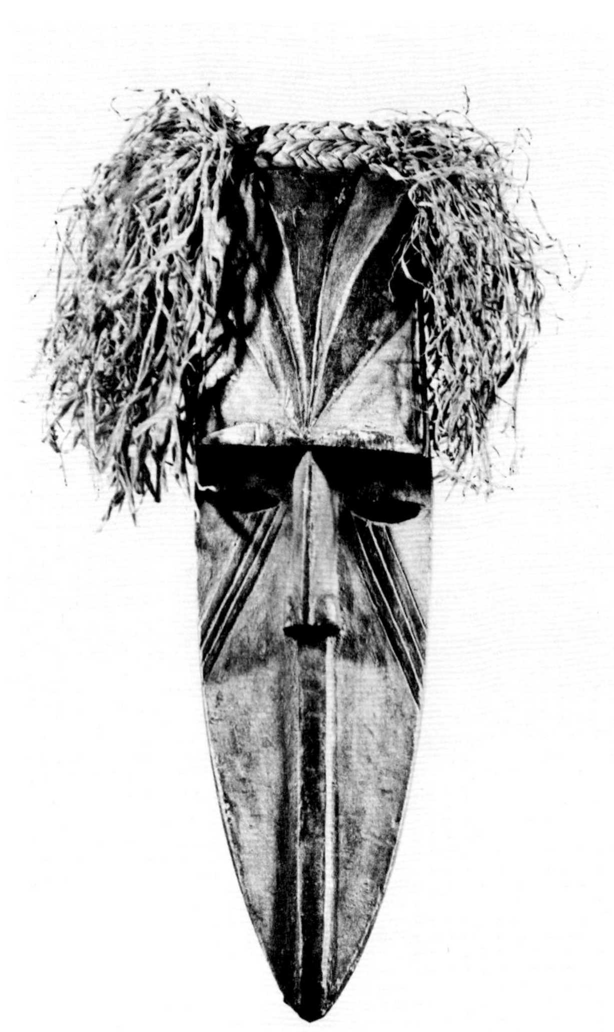

71. FACE MASK (*IGRI*)

Igbo, Afikpo subgroup
Wood, raffia, pigment h. 15½″
Lent by William Arnett

The Afikpo Igbo (population 35,000) live on the west bank of the Cross River in the eastern portion of Igbo territory. Many types of masks are used by the Afikpo in a yearly cycle of plays and dances.

The *Okumkpa* is the most popular Afikpo masquerade. It is performed by men's society members and consists of large groups of masked players performing satirical and topical skits.

This mask type is uncommon and is usually worn by adult men who may act as dancers, singers or musicians. *Igri* masqueraders wear floppy, broad brimmed hats or the standard musician's costume of khaki shirt and shorts. The igri is also known as *okonkpo* or *egede*.

Wittmer and Arnett, 1978. p. 32, ill. cat no. 72.
Ottenberg, 1975. pp. 3-15, 24-27.

Cross River

In the densely forested area of the Cross River live peoples who speak Bantoid languages. This region is the only area of the world where wooden masks are covered with skin. Other Cross River stylistic characteristics are the frequent use of cap headdresses and double-headed janus forms.

Peoples whose art is considered typically Cross River in style include the Ejagham (population 90,000) and related Akparabong of the middle Cross River and The Boki (population 90,000) of the middle or upper Cross River. Bordering the Cross River to the west are the Ibibio (population 1,500,000 including the related Ogoni and Oron) and some Igbo groups. The Ogoni occupy the area between the Cross River and the Niger Delta and are culturally and linguistically related to the Ibibio.

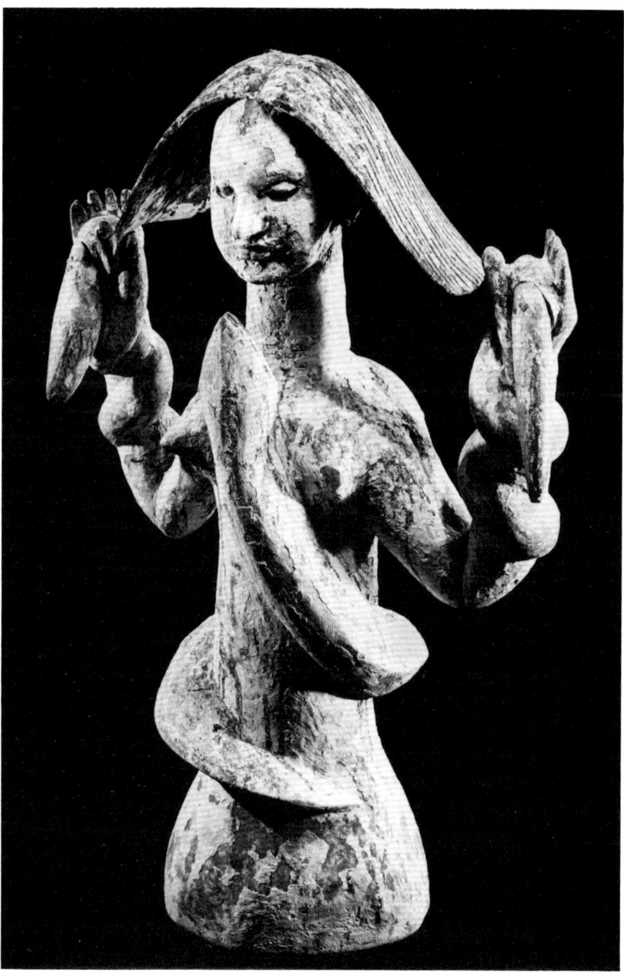

74. SHRINE FIGURE (MAMMY WATA)
Ibibio, Annang
Wood, pigment, h. 34½″
Lent by William Arnett

Peoples of the Niger Delta and Cross River areas share the widespread belief in spirits that dwell deep in the waters and which have beneficial as well as destructive aspects. Mammy Wata is the general name for these water spirits. Mammy Wata spirits are depicted as beautiful, light-skinned and having long, European-type hair. Sometimes they are shown wreathed in snakes or having the tail of a mermaid. Carved representations of these spirits in the form of humans is a fairly recent innovation and has been prevalent in the Ibibio area for only thirty to forty years. Iconography used in representations of this spirit is thought to have been strongly influenced by a popular imported German print of a snake charmer.

Wittmer and Arnett, 1978. p. 62. ill. pl. 144, front cover
Salmons, 1977. pp. 8-15, 87-88.

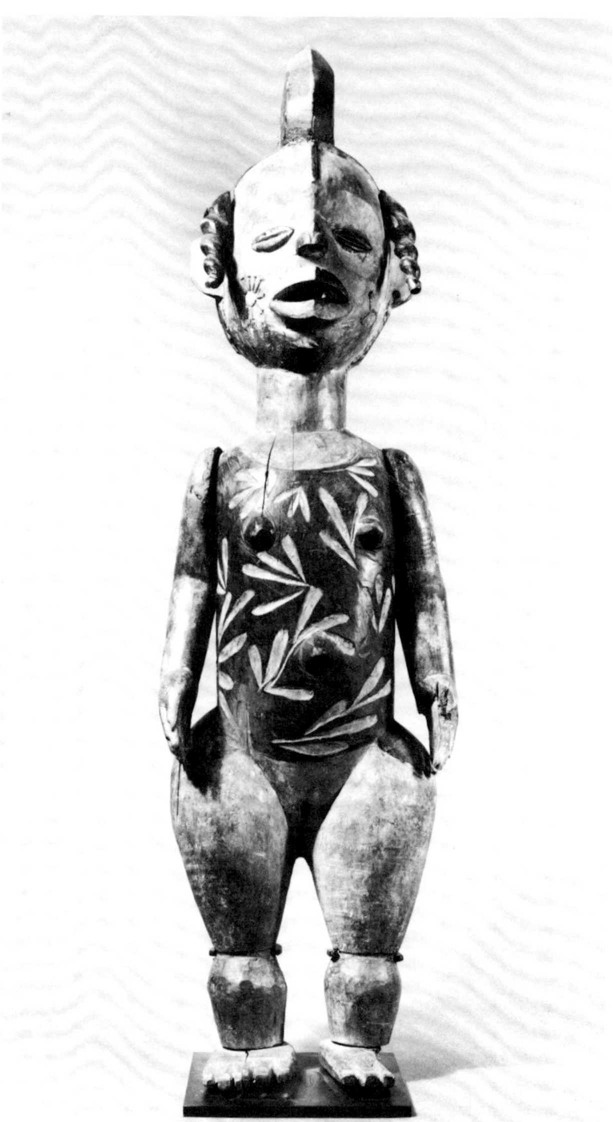

75. PUPPET
Ibibio
Wood, h. 24″
Lent by Leonard and Judith Kahan

The *Ekon* Society of the Ibibio uses puppets in plays which both entertain and offer social criticism. This piece has moveable arms and resembles these puppets. It does not, however, portray any of the standard types represented by Ekon society figures, and its function is unknown.

Mount, 1983. ill., cat no. 34.
Scheinberg, 1977.

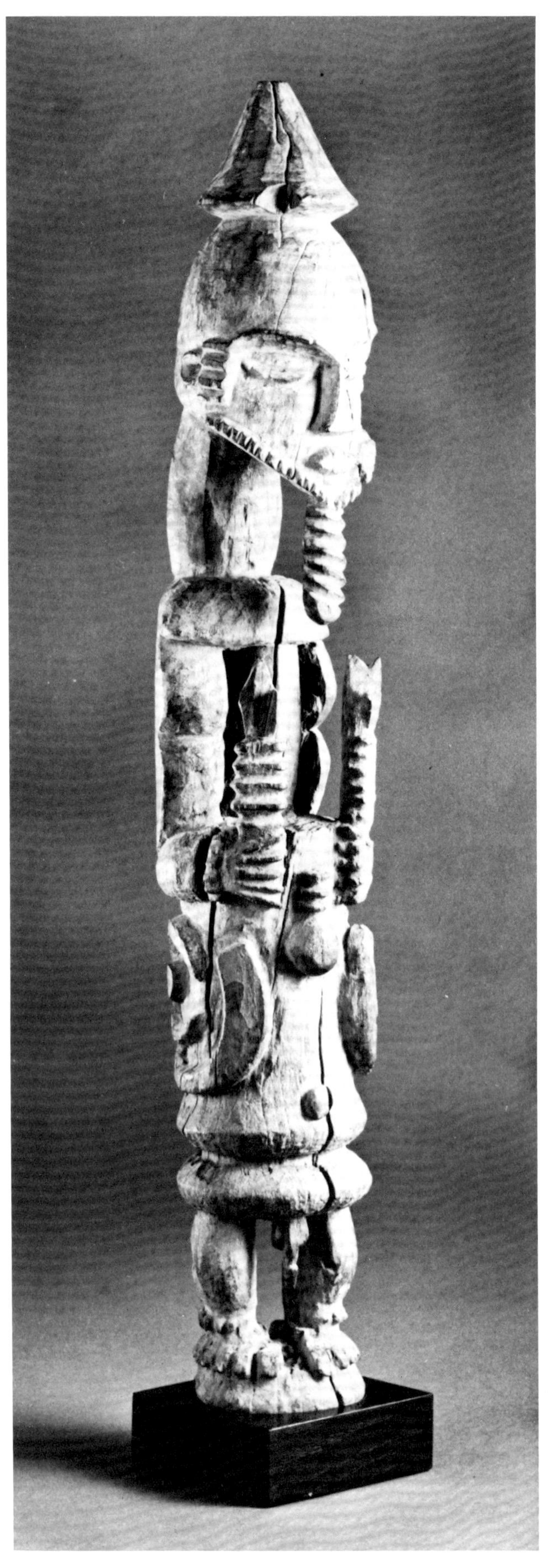

76

77

76. STANDING MALE FIGURE (*EKPU*)
Oron Ibibio
Wood, h. 26⅞″
Eighteenth-nineteenth centuries
Private collection

Although ancestors are revered throughout Africa, fewer sculptural representations of ancestors are made than were once supposed. Carved figurative ancestor representations do exist, however, and included in this group are *ekpu* made by the Oron, a small group associated with the Ibibio. Ekpu represent specific male ancestors and serve as repositories for their spirits. The size and elaborateness of the carving depended on the wealth and status of the deceased. A female ancestor was represented by a pot and a child or junior member of a family by a plain stick. The figures were kept in a special building called *obio* and received periodic sacrifices of food and wine. Ekpu figures have not been made since the early twentieth century and are among the oldest surviving African wood carvings.

Leuzinger, 1960. ill. pl. 34.
Murray, 1948. pp. 310-314.
Lunsford, 1975. p. 96.

77. FACE MASK (*ELU*)
Ogoni
Wood, pigment, h. 11¼″
The Milton D. Ratner Family Collection

The Ogoni, who live between the lower Niger and Cross River regions, have graded masking societies which serve various functions. Small *elu* masks are worn by young men. These masks have delicately carved human faces and hinged, articulated jaws containing teeth made of split bamboo. The mouths are manipulated by the wearers of these masks and their technique is kept secret from those who are not members of the masking society. The masks are attached to a conical raffia and cloth cap and are worn with a cloth costume. The hairdo in this example forms a graceful shape resembling animal horns.

Drewal, 1977. p. 48, ill. pl. 47.

78. FACE MASK (*ELU*)
Ogoni
Wood, pigment, h. 9½″
Private collection

Elu masks are usually painted black and white. This example shows evidence of many repaintings.

79. ANTELOPE FACE-MASK (*KARIKPO*)
Ogoni
Wood, pigment h. 18½″
Lent by William Arnett

Ceremonies honoring a local founding ancestor are held by the Ogoni at the beginning of the farming season. A graceful, acrobatic dance is performed by a dancer wearing an antelope mask (*karikpo*). He is joined by a dancer wearing a mask which falls in the ugly or beast tradition and who dances in an appropriately wild manner.

Wittmer and Arnett, 1978 p. 48, ill. p. 49, cat no. 120.

80. ANTELOPE FACE-MASK (*KARIKPO*)
Ogoni
Wood, pigment h. 15¼″
Lent by William Arnett

Wittmer and Arnett, 1978. ill. p. 49, cat no. 121.

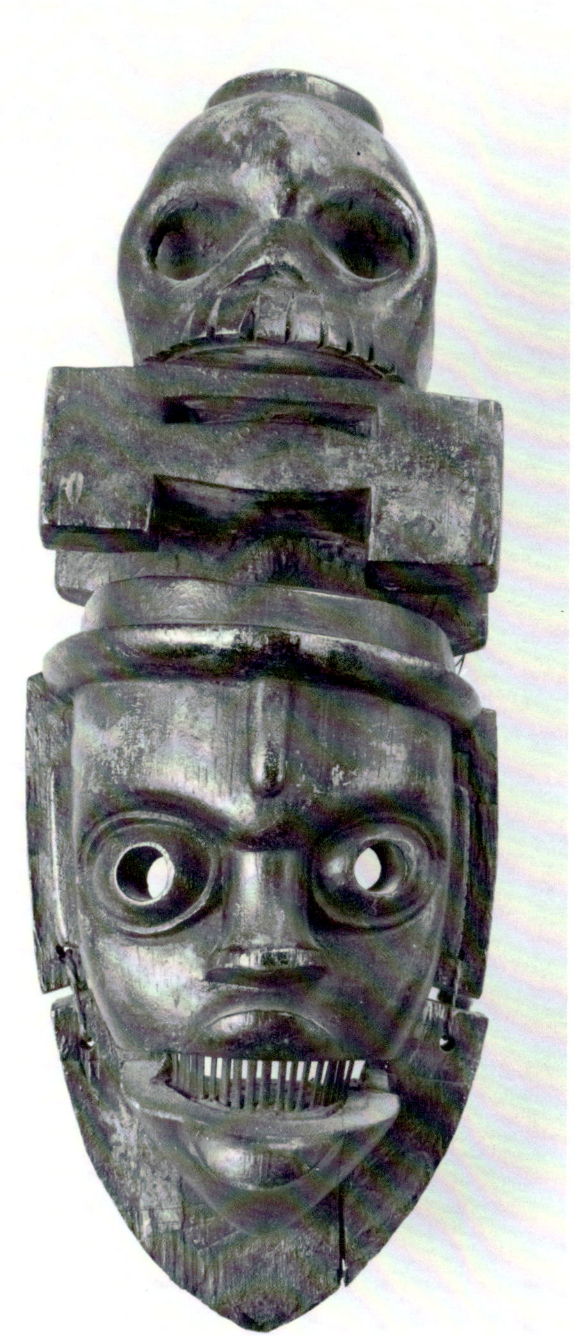

81. FACE MASK (*ZIM*)
Ogoni
Wood, h. 12¼″
The Seattle Art Museum, Katherine White Collection, 81.17.536

The theme of duality is shown in this mask by a skull carved above a human face with an articulated jaw. This probably falls in the catagory of *zim* or anti-aesthetic masks used in conjunction with either the elu or karikpo types, both of which are considered aesthetically pleasing. Thompson attributes this mask to the Gokana Ogoni on the basis of K. C. Murray's unpublished field notes.

Thompson, 1963. ill. pl. J-1, p. 130. and unpublished note to Katherine White, n.d.
Wittmer and Arnett, 1978. p. 47.
Drewal, 1977. p. 48.

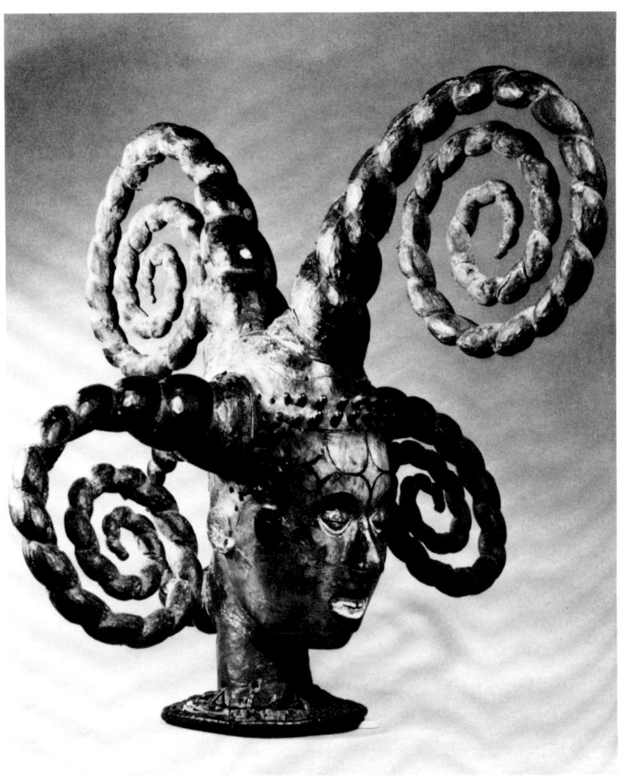

82. CAP HEADDRESS
Ejagham, Obubra Division, Abekele
Wood, skin, basketry, h. 26″
Lent by Hugh and Ida Kohlmeyer

The origin of the use of skin-covered masks and headdresses in the Cross River area is uncertain. There is speculation that the practice originated with the wearing of trophy heads of slain enemies. Although some authorities claim that in the past the carved wooden headdresses were covered with human skin, little documentation for this exists. The use of these masks is believed to have originated among the Ejagham (Ekoi). Field observations indicate that the masks are covered with freshly killed antelope skin. Headdresses are attached to basketry caps which are secured by a cord under the wearer's chin and are worn with a long gown that covers his head and body.

This light-faced, naturalistic headdress represents a female. Horn-like spirals and wooden pegs indicate hair. Raised keloid ethnic marks which are characteristic of the Cross River region appear at the temples, and dark markings of vegetable pigments adorn the cheeks and forehead. The cheek pattern is a mark of *nsibidi*, the ancient symbolic script of the Ejagham. Such symbols were sometimes tatooed on the cheeks of Cross River peoples.

Niklin, 1974. pp. 8-15, 67-68.
Thompson, 1974. p. 175-188.

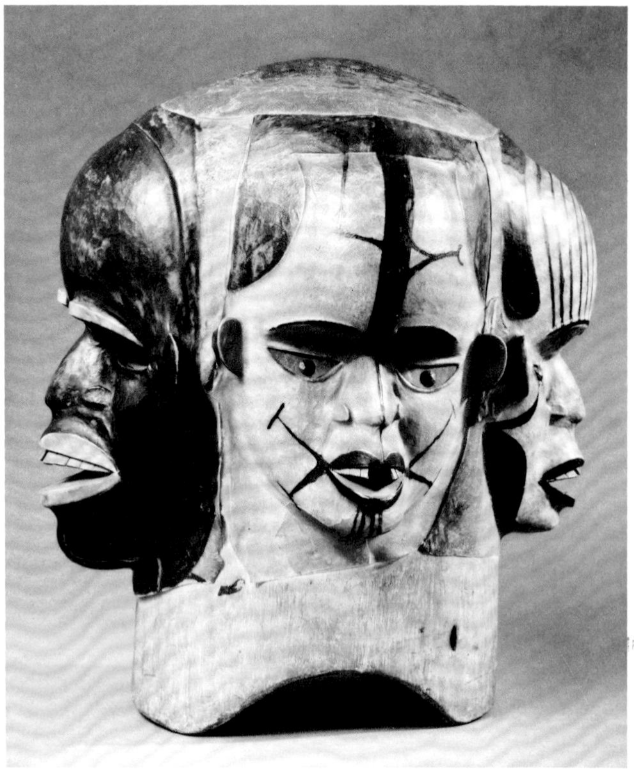

83. FOUR-FACED HELMET MASK
Ejagham, Akparabong area
Wood, skin, h. 16″
The Paul and Ruth Tishman Collection

In addition to headcrests, janus or multi-faced skin covered helmet masks are found in the Cross River area of Nigeria and Cameroon. Masks are owned and used by masking associations of restricted membership and perform at important occasions such as initiations and funerals. In performance, helmet masks are worn with cloth costumes and are sometimes decorated with feathers.

The darker brown faces are said to be male while the lighter ones are female. Janus and multi-faced masks are the most prestigious Cross River headdresses and are usually owned by associations whose members are wealthy and of high status. The chipped teeth, linear facial painting and shiny oiled surfaces are signs of beauty and civilization.

Niklin attributes this mask to the carver, Takim Eyuk, who died in 1915. Today, mask associations are declining in importance or are no longer in existence, and few skin-covered masks are being made.

Niklin in Vogel, ed., 1981, pp. 173-174, ill. pl. 103, p. 173.
Niklin, 1974. pp. 8-15, 67-68.
Blier, 1980. p. 14.
Anton, et al., 1979. ill. cover.

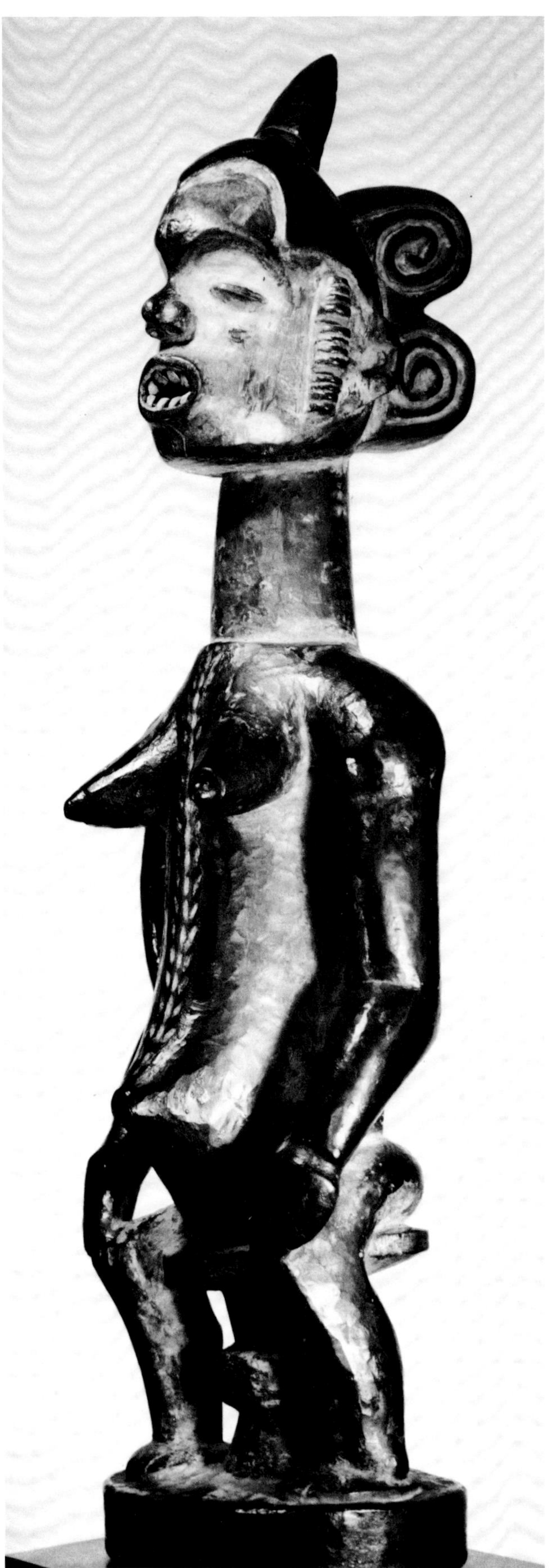

85

84. CAP HEADDRESS
Boki

Wood, cloth bamboo, metal, fiber, teeth, pigment, h. 15″
The Milton D. Ratner Family Collection

The Boki make both skin covered masks and masks without skin covering. They are used by masking associations which formerly played a significant part in many aspects of Boki life. The major women's association, *egbege*, had an important role and controlled the fattening house, an institution for the education and beautification of prospective brides. Egbege masks have tall hairdos, and Henry Drewal attributes this janiform headdress to this association. He states that it may represent an earlier and distinctive Boki style. Although owned by a female association, the mask was worn by a male.

The materials attached to this janus cap headdress intensify its effectiveness by incorporating elements of wealth (brass, fiber, embroidered cloth), strength (teeth), and the sacred (the linear patterns on the headdress and neck which resemble the sacred nsibidi script used by several Cross River peoples).

H. Drewal, 1977, p. 46, ill. pl. 46 a, b, pp. 46-47
Niklin, 1974. pp. 8-15, 67-68.
Thompson, 1974. pp. 177-181.

85. SEATED FEMALE FIGURE
Ibibio/Eket or **Idoma/Igala**

Wood, pigment, h. 37″
The Milton D. Ratner Family Collection

Seated female figures of this style have appeared in several publications with differing attributions. Although the southern Ibibio town of Eket is suggested for similar pieces, it may also be possible that the origin of this figure is the Idoma or Igala peoples who live north of the Ibibio. The Idoma use seated wooden figures which represent bush or water spirits and have curative and fertility enhancing powers. A carved female figure may also be placed next to the bodies of old men at their funerals.

The uncertainty concerning the origin of this piece indicates the artistic interchange and influence which exists among nearby ethnic groups.

Schadler, 1976. cf. pl. VI, pp. 84-85.
Wittmer and Arnett. 1978. cf. pl. 137, p. 57.
Siroto, 1976. cf. pl. 108, p. 58.
Sieber, 1961. p. 9-10, 23.

Nigerian Plateau

Many of the people of northeastern Nigeria practice Islam and no longer make figurative sculpture. Rich sculptural traditions continue for many peoples of the upper Benue River area or Nigerian Plateau. These groups live largely in compact farming villages. Most settlements are small, and only the Jukun developed a complex state. Represented in this exhibition from the upper Benue area are the Chamba (population 20,000), the Tiv (population 800,000), the Mumuye (population 70,000), the Montol (population 10,000), the Yergum (population 35,000), the Mama (population 8,000), the Jukun (population 40,000), and the Mambila (population 20,000).

The Idoma (population 250,000), Igala (population 200,000), and Afo (population 8,000) live near the confluence of the Niger and Benue Rivers and speak related Kwa languages. Their art styles form a bridge between the art of the Igbo and the styles of the Nigerian Plateau.

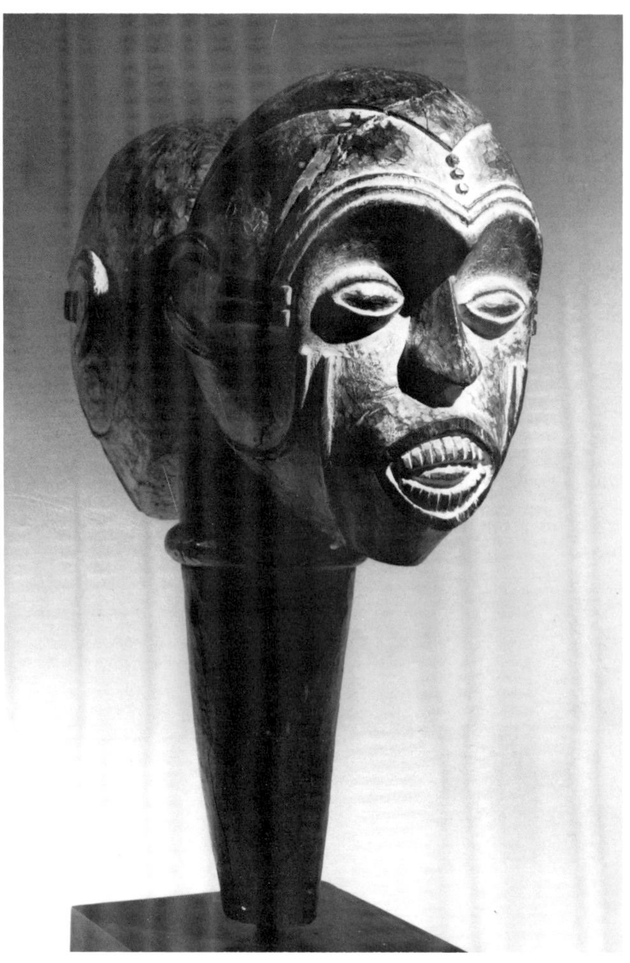

86. HEADCREST (?)
Idoma
Wood, pigment, h. 17⅘″
Lent by Leonard and Judith Kahan

Among the Idoma, men's societies based on age sets function as mutual aid clubs for funerals and as dance guilds. Masks are used as symbolic representations of the whole men's society. Although the secrets of masks are kept from women, masks may perform divination for them.

This janus-headed object may have been used as a headcrest and inserted into a basketry cap. A similar piece has been attributed to the *Oglinye* Association.

Armstrong, 1970. pp. 98-100.
S. Kasfir cited in Lamp, 1983. p. 46.

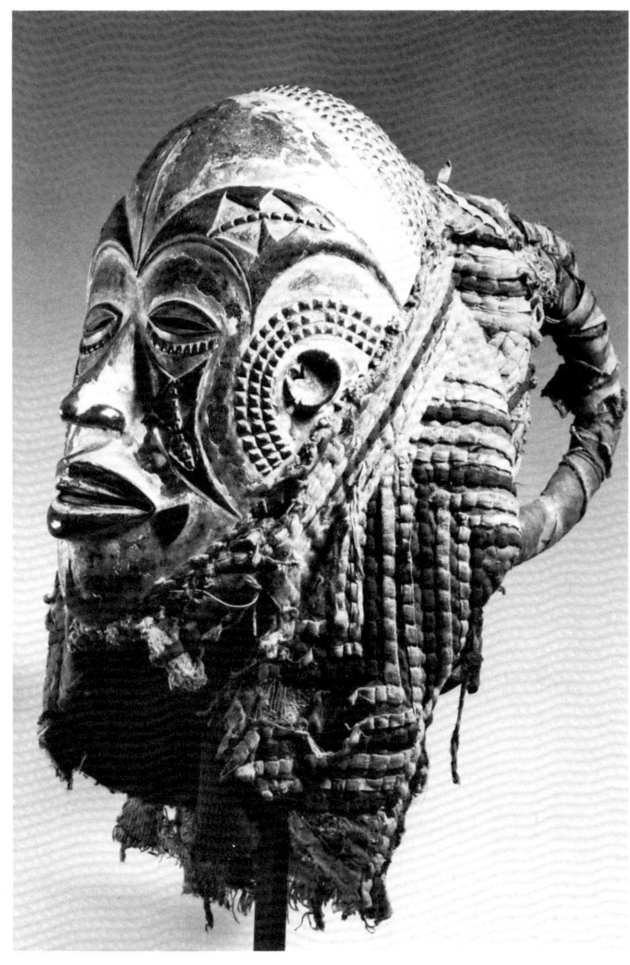

87. FACE MASK
Igala, Cross River State, village of Ip Ipum
Wood, pigment, cloth, h. 12″
Lent by Charles and Kent Davis

According to Roy Sieber, the Igala have imported mask types, dances and music from the Igbo. Unlike traditional Igala masks, these are secular and are not treated with the secrecy and respect that are shown Igala masks associated with religious activities. Both the Igala and the Igbo use masquerades to dramatize the relationship between the world of the ancestors and the world of the living. Among the Igbo, masquerades such as the white-faced mmuo depict the ancestors in a generalized way. While this generalized type is used by the Igala, masquerades portraying individual ancestors also appear. The appliqué costume attached to this mask relates to both Igbo and northern Edo masquerade dress (see cat nos. 55 and 66). Another cultural similarity the Igala share with the Igbo is the use of ikenga. (cat nos. 59 and 60)

Boston, 1977. p. 18.
Sieber, 1961, p. 6.

88. HEADDRESS
Afo
Wood, skin, pigment, basketry, h. 27″
Lent by Charles and Kent Davis

This janus-faced headdress is topped by a figure riding a bicycle. Riding figures connote speed and power. The white painted wheels repeat the forms of the paired faces.

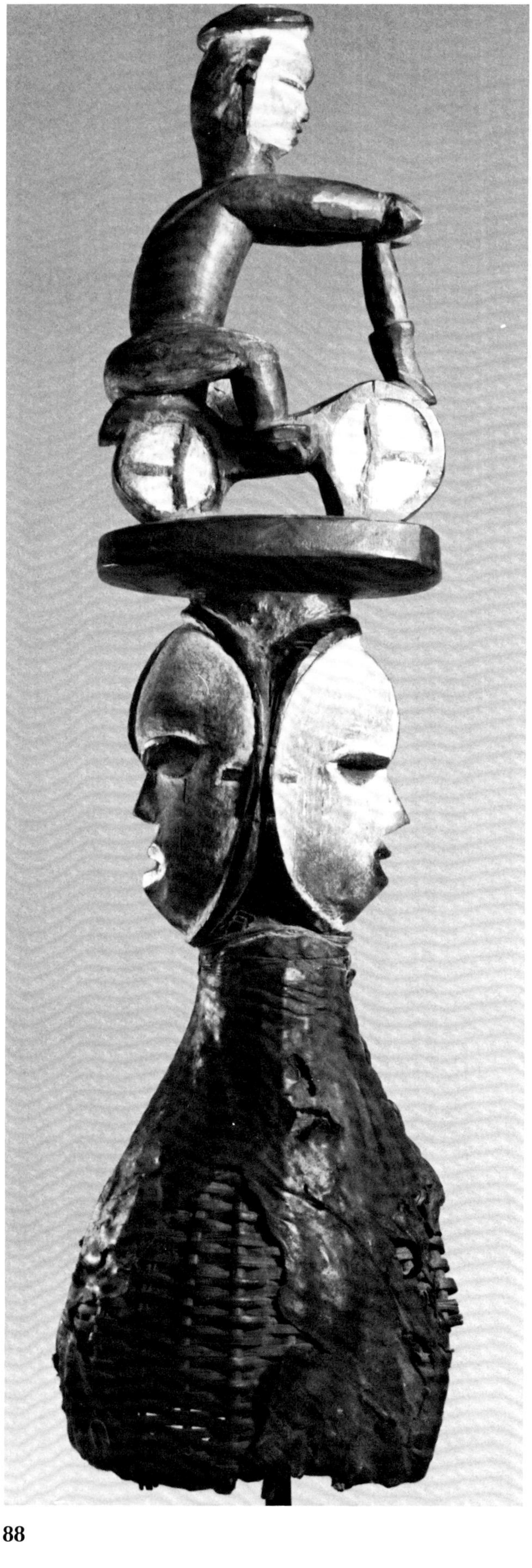

88

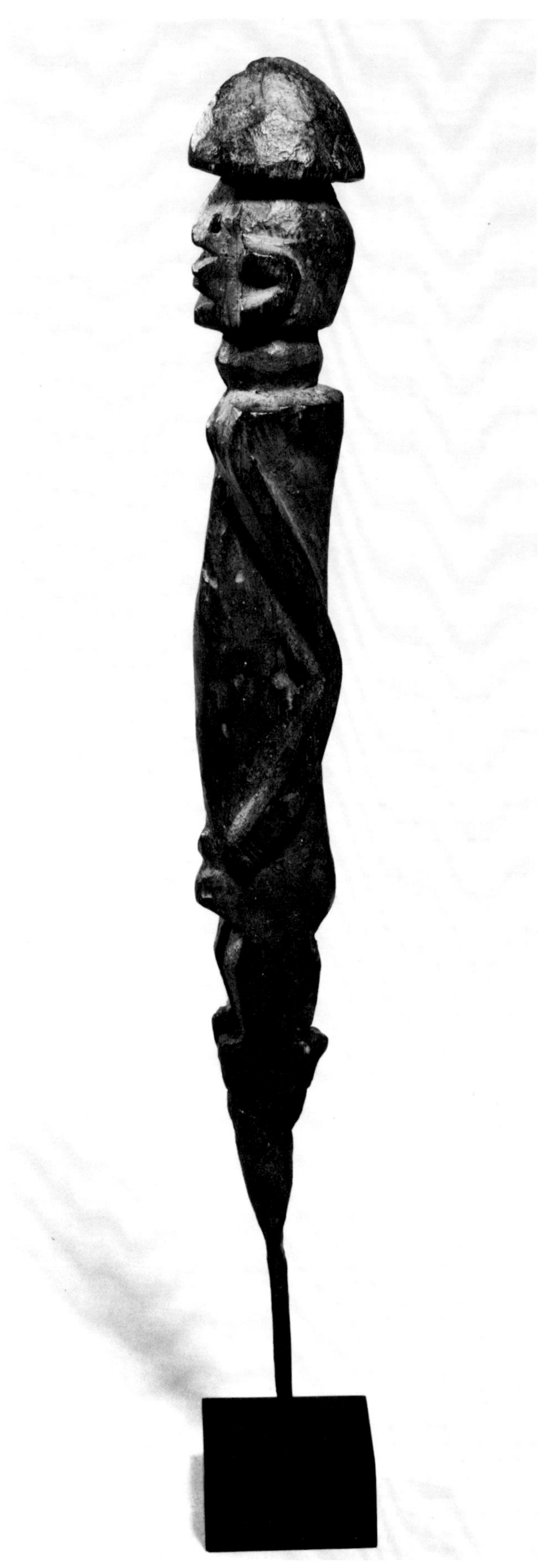

89

89. PROTECTIVE FIGURE (*TAU-KENDOA*)
Chamba
Wood, iron, h. 13″
Birmingham Museum of Art, gift of Margaret Pennington in honor of her mother, Mrs. Regina Kirchoff Mandrell 1984.59

Slender, cylindrical wooden figures made by the Chamba were described by Frobinius in the early years of this century as being used to protect villagers against snake bite and in agricultural celebrations. The figures can appear as pairs consisting of a male and a female as well as singly. The female figures (*tau-kendoa*) have a flat cap or hair treatment while the male's cap is pointed. The pointed iron base was inserted into the ground.

Similar figures with a tall crest are made by the Wurkun, another Benue River group, as well as by the Junkun and Mambila. A pole-like quality and a simple, severe geometry is characteristic of the sculpture of the peoples of this region.

Frobinius cited in Roy, 1979. p. 57.
Sieber and Vevers, 1974. np.

90. PROTECTIVE FIGURE
Chamba
Wood, h. 21″
Lent by Robert and Nancy Nooter

The Chamba revere twins, and double figures are made to protect them from death. Figures such as these may also be placed either inside or outside a dwelling for protection.

Scheinberg, 1975. p. 28
Seligman and Berin, 1982. p. 38.
Gillon, 1979. ill. p. 79, pl. 84.

91. STANDING FIGURE
Mumuye
Wood, pigment, h. 46″
New Orleans Museum of Art, gift of Victor K. Kiam

The Mumuye use carved figures in the context of rainmaking, healing, protection, reinforcing the status of elders and for greeting visitors to the village. They also have a judicial function and may be used both to discern the identity of thieves and to determine veracity at trials. A particular figure cannot be correlated with a function on the basis of its appearance or size, and carvings may have more than one function.

The angularity and elongated form of these figures show relationships to figurative carvings of peoples of the Western Sudan. Sculpture made in the Benue River area may be considered the southern most extention of this stylistic approach. The figures do not possess identifying gender characteristics; however, the rectangular forms on the head may refer to the stretched earlobes of Mumuye women.

Roy, 1979. p. 59
Rubin in Vogel, ed., 1981. pp. 155-158.

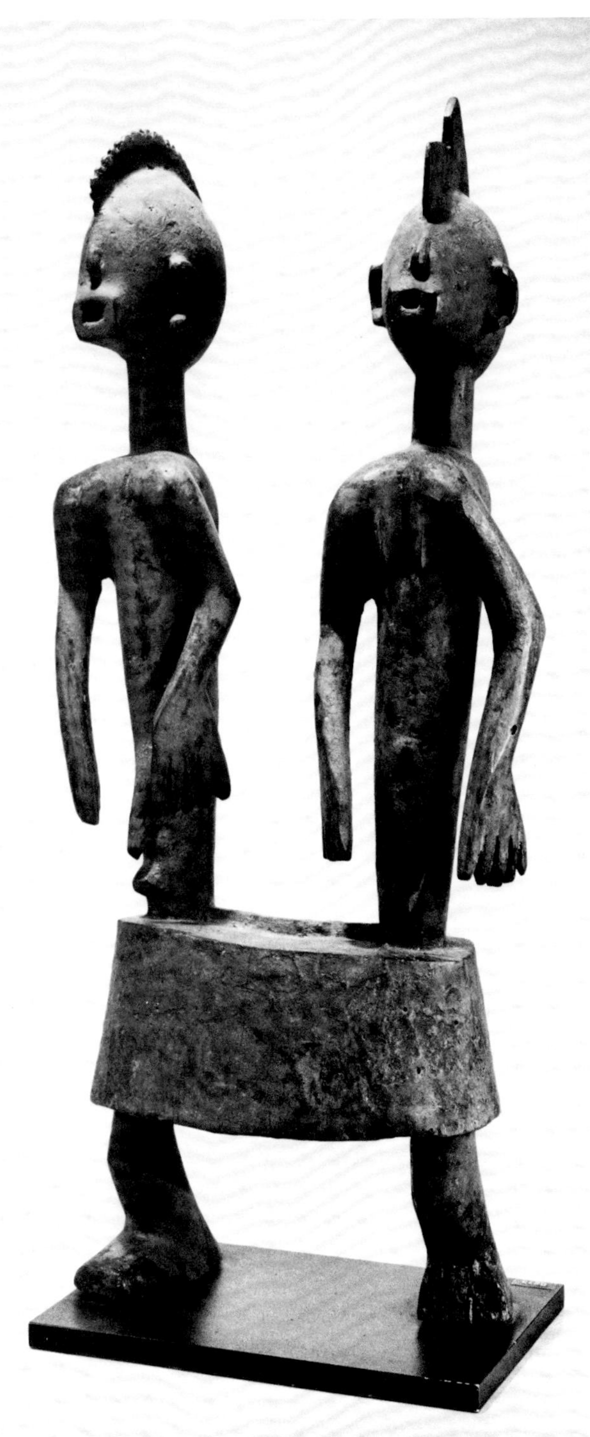

90

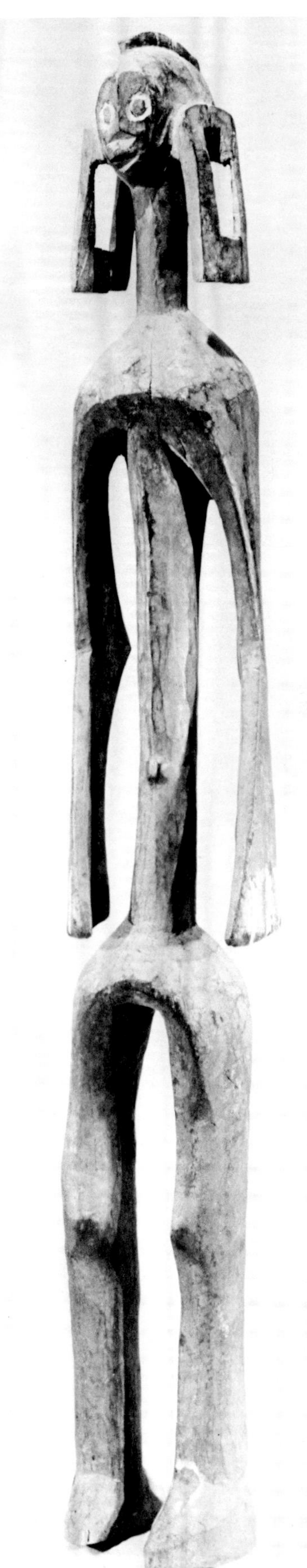

91

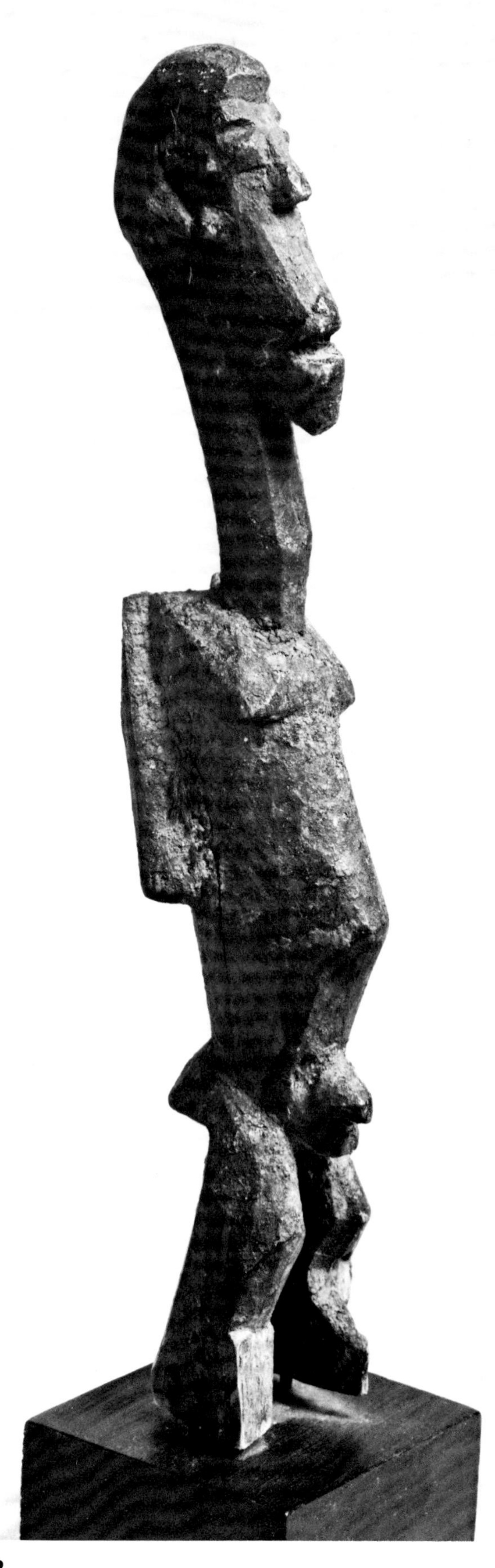

92

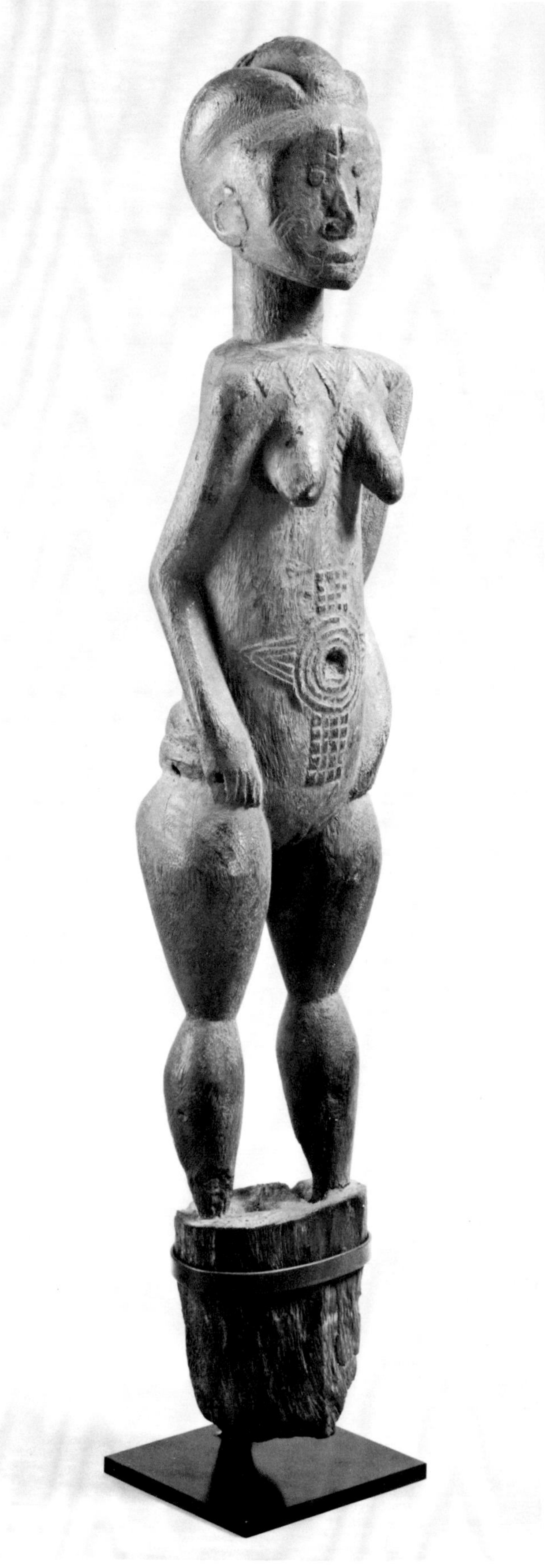

93

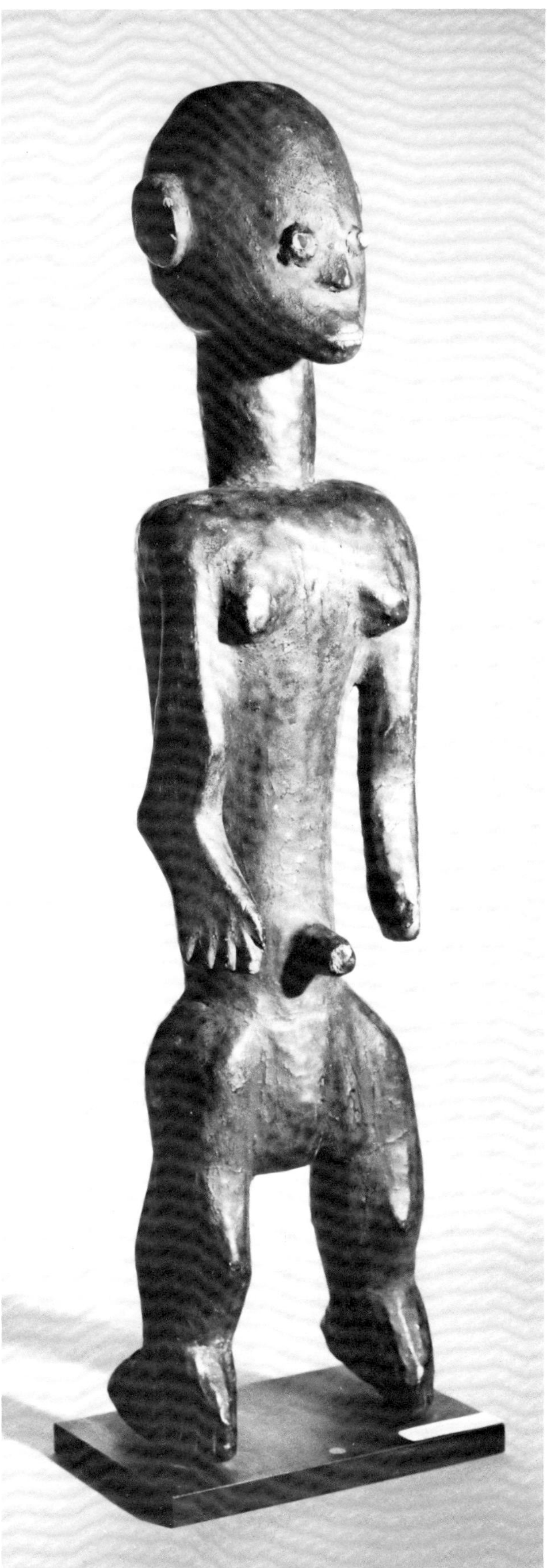

94

92. FIGURE
Montol
Wood, patination, h. 10½″
Lent by Dr. John Nixon

The Montol use figure carvings for the men's *Komtin* society. Their primary function is in rites associated with curing. The Montol and other peoples of this area sometimes use carvings made by neighboring ethnic groups, and Montol carvings have been observed in use by the Goemai to the west.

Sieber, 1961. p. 9.

93. FEMALE FIGURE (*ATSUKU*)
Tiv
Wood, h. 30″
High Museum of Art, Atlanta, Georgia, Fred and Rita Richman Collection 72.40.234

The Tiv live on both sides of the Benue River. Carved wooden female figures attached to posts are called *atsuku* and serve functions relating to hunting and circumcision rites. They have been associated symbolically with virility.

Hersey, 1973. ill. plate 9, p. 17.
Wittmer and Arnett, 1978. p. 96.

94. STANDING FIGURE
Yergum (?)
Wood, patination, h. 19¾″
The Milton D. Ratner Family Collection

Among the Yergum and other northeastern Jukun-speaking peoples, carved figures represent deceased chiefs and attendant figures and are the focus for veneration. They may also serve a protective function.

Drewal, 1977. p. 53, ill. pl. 54.

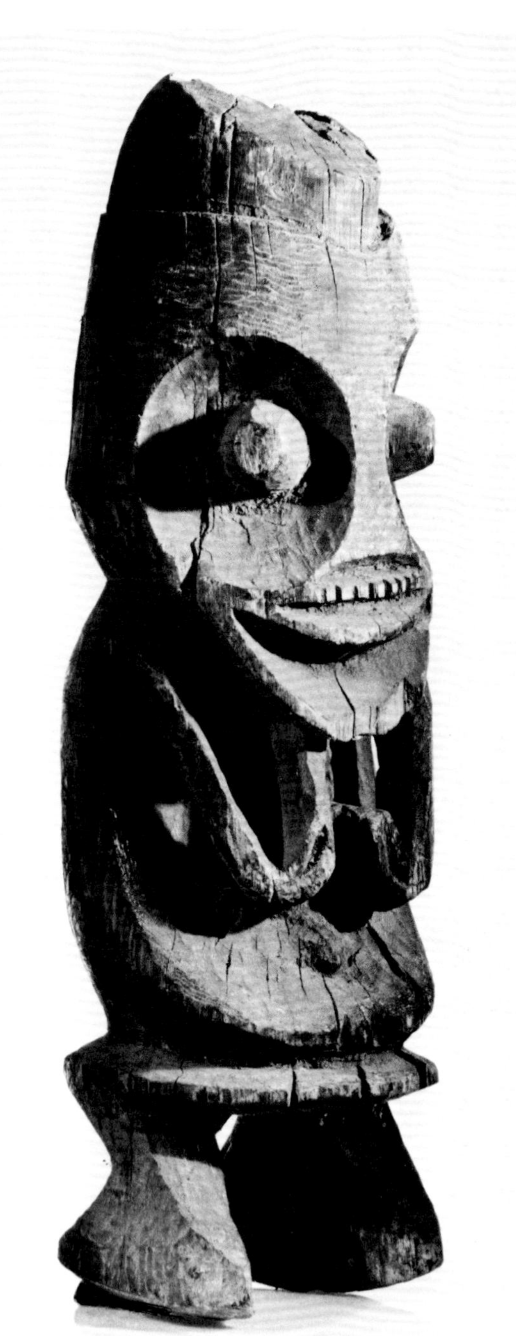

95. MALE FIGURE (*TADEP DUA*)
Mambila
Wood, h. 22″
Lent by Wiliam Arnett

The Mambila occupy hilly country in eastern Nigeria and across the border in neighboring Cameroon. Ancestor figures known as *tadep* are made from wood or raffia palm pith. They are painted red, white and black and sometimes take the form of a joined male-female pair. The figures are not named for specific ancestors. Tatep are kept in an ancestral or storage hut for ceremonial objects. Figures are allowed to decay and are not retrieved if they fall. They are only expected to last about a year and are replaced when necessary.

Wittmer and Arnett, 1978. ill. p. 85, pl. 204.
Schwartz, n.d.

96. FEMALE FIGURE
Mambila
Clay, red pigment h. 11¾″
Lent by William Arnett

Fertility figures are made in clay by the Mambila. This figure may have been used in this manner or it may have had a protective function.

Wittmer and Arnett, 1978. ill. p. 108, pl. 254.
Schwartz, n.d., p. 23-24.

97. FIGURE
Mambila
Clay, h. 9½″
Lent by William Arnett

Wittmer and Arnett, 1978. ill. p. 108, pl. 252.

98. BUSH COW HELMET MASK
Chamba
Wood, pigment, l. 25″
The Milton D. Ratner Family Collection

Horizontal horned masks representing powerful, aggressive bush cows are used widely by groups living in the vicinity of the Benue River. This mask was worn by a member of a men's secret society known as *Vara* in a funerary context. Masks of this type also function to protect humans and crops and perform at secret society initiations. The wearer is dressed in a full fiber costume and is sometimes accompanied by a female partner.

H. Drewal, 1977. p. 51, ill. pl. 51.
Sieber and Vevers, 1974. cf. cat no. 17.

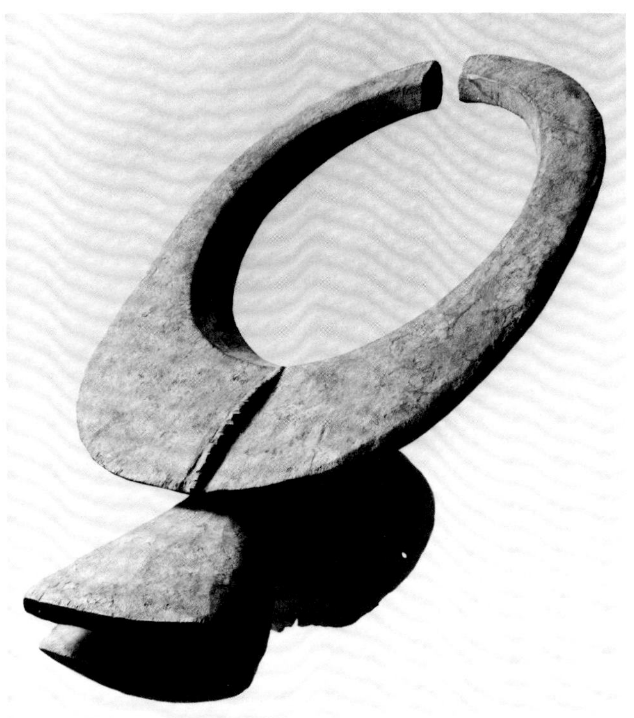

99. BUSH COW HEADDRESS
Mama
Wood, l. 17″
The Milton D. Ratner Family Collection

The *Magam* cult of the Mama uses several types of horned headdresses in agricultural ceremonies and funerals. The Mama, who live north of the Benue River, are known for their prowess in the arts of war. These masks are danced with forceful and threatening movements. The Mama believe masked figures wearing costumes of dried grasses represent the returned dead.

H. Drewal, 1977. pp. 50-51, ill. pl. 50.
Sieber and Vevers, 1974. cf. pl. 14.
Rubin, 1970. p. 112.

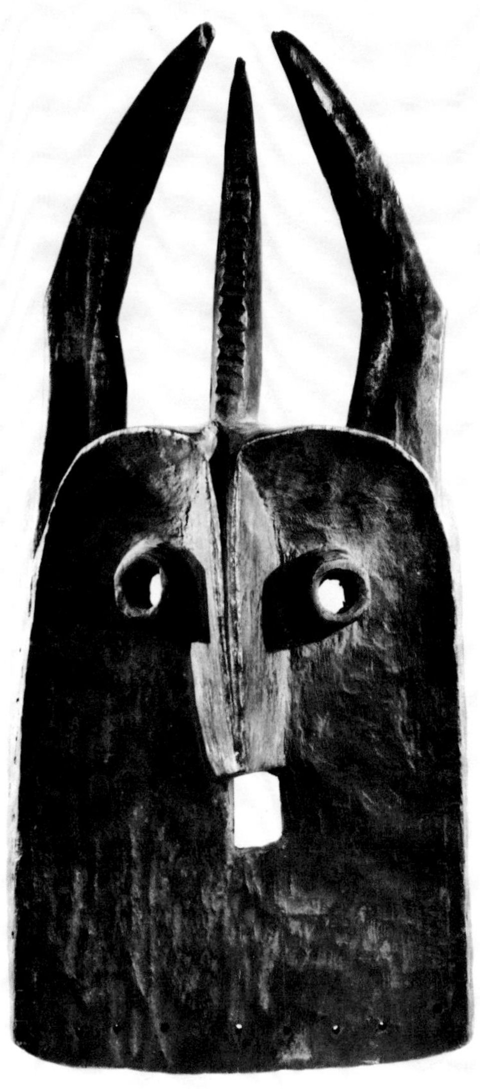

100. MASK (*AKUMA WA'UNU*)
Jukun
Wood, h. 29″
Lent by Leonard and Judith Kahan

The Jukun, unlike most peoples of the Nigerian Plateau, developed a complex state. The Jukun kingdom expanded in the seventeenth century and, after a period of decline, was conquered by the Fulani in the early nineteenth century.

This large, highly geometricized face mask is part of the wide spread tradition of bush animal representations. It is of the type known as *akuma wa'unu*. Masks for the *Akuma* cult are danced in male and female pairs; the male is carved of wood and the female is made of netted fiber. Male masks are worn tipped at a thirty degree angle from the vertical with a cloth or palm frond costume and a black raffia cape. This mask type functions primarily to drive away witchcraft and to insure a good harvest.

Mount, 1983. ill. cat no. 97.
Rubin, 1970. pp. 66-70. cf. cat no. 77.

Bibliography

A Catalog of a Collection of Benin Works of Art. London: Sotheby Parke Bernet and Co., 1980.

Adams, Monni. *Designs for Living.* Cambridge: Harvard University Press, 1982.

__________. "Sacred Children: Twins in the Ritual and Art of the Yoruba of Nigeria." *Symbols.* Winter 1980: 2-3, 11.

Anton, et. al. *Primitive Art.* New York: Harry N. Abrams, 1979.

Arinze, Francis. *Sacrifice in Igbo Religion.* Ibadan: Ibadan University Press, 1979.

Armstrong, Robert G., *The Idoma-Speaking Peoples.* Ethnographic Survey of Africa, Part X. London: International African Institute, 1955, reprinted 1970.

__________. *The Igala.* Ethnographic Survey of Africa, Part X. London: International African Institute, 1955, reprinted 1970.

Awonlalu, J. Omosade. *Yoruba Beliefs and Sacrificial Rites.* London: Longmans, 1979.

Balandier, G., and J. Maquet. *Dictionary of Black African Civilization.* New York: Leon Amiel, 1974.

Barber, Karin. "How Man Makes God in West Africa: Yoruba Attitudes Toward the Orisa." *Africa.* 51(3): 724-44 (1981).

Bascom, William. *African Arts.* Berkley: University of California, 1967.

__________. *African Art in Cultural Perspective, an Introduction.* New York: W.W. Norton and Company, 1973.

__________. *The Yoruba of Southwestern Nigeria.* New York: Holt, Rinehart and Winston, 1969.

Ben-Amos, Paula. "Ekpo Ritual in Avbiama Village." *African Arts.* 2(4): 8-13, 79.

__________. *The Art of Benin.* London: Thames and Hudson, 1980.

Ben-Amos, Paula and Arnold Rubin, ed. *The Art of Power/The Power of Art-Studies in Benin Iconography.* Los Angeles: Museum of Cultural History, 1983.

Berns, Marla. *Agbaye: Yoruba Art in Context.* Los Angeles: Museum of Cultural History, 1979.

Blier, Susan. *Africa's Cross River, Art of the Nigerian-Cameroon Border Redefined.* New York: L. Kahan Gallery, 1980.

__________. *Beauty and the Beast.* New York: Tribal Arts Gallery Two, 1976.

__________. *Gestures in African Art.* New York: L. Kahan Gallery, 1982.

Bohannan, Paul. "Beauty and Scarification Among the Tiv." *Man.* 56(129): 117-121 (1956).

Borgatti, Jean. *From the Hands of Lawrence Ajanaku.* Los Angeles: University of California, 1979.

Boston, J. S. *Ikenga.* London: Ethnographica, 1977.

__________. "Some Northern Ibo Masquerades." *The Journal of the Royal Anthropological Institute of Great Britain and Ireland.* 90: 54-65 (1960).

Bradbury, R. E. *Benin Studies.* New York: International African Institute, 1973.

__________. *The Benin Kingdom and the Edo-Speaking Peoples of Southwestern Nigeria.* Ethnographic Survey of Africa, Part XIII. London: International African Institute, 1957, reprinted 1970.

Cole, Herbert M. *African Arts of Transformation.* Santa Barbara: University of California, 1970.

__________. "Art is a Verb in Iboland." *African Arts.* 3(1): 34-41 (1969c).

__________. "Mbari is Life." *African Arts.* 2(3): 8-17, 87 (1969a).

__________. "Mbari is a Dance." *African Arts.* 3(4): 42-51, 79 (1969b).

__________. *Mbari: Art and Life Among the Owerri Igbo.* Bloomington: Indiana University Press, 1982.

Courlander, Harold. *Tales of Yoruba Gods and Heroes.* Greenwich, CT: Fawcett, 1973.

Dark, Philip J. C. *The Art of Benin.* Chicago: Chicago Natural History Museum, 1962.

Drewal, Henry J. *African Artistry, Technique and Aesthetics in Yoruba Sculpture.* Atlanta: High Museum of Art, 1980.

__________. "The Arts of the Egungun Among the Yoruba People." *African Arts.* 11(3): 18-19 (1978).

__________. *Traditional Art of the Nigerian People.* Washington, D.C.: Museum of African Art, 1977.

Drewal, Henry J. and Margaret T. Drewal. *Gelede, Art and Female Power Among the Yoruba.* Bloomington: Indiana University Press, 1983.

Drewal, Margaret T. "Projections from the Top in Yoruba Art." *African Arts.* 11(1): 43-49, 91-92 (1977).

Drewal, Margaret T. and Henry J. "Gelede Dance of the Western Yoruba." *African Arts.* 8(2): 36-49, 78-79 (1975).

Ebin, Victoria. *The Body Decorated.* London: Thames and Hudson, 1979.

Eyo, Ekpo. *Two Thousand Years of Nigerian Art.* Lagos: Federal Department of Antiquities, 1974.

Eyo, Ekpo and Willett, Frank. *Treasures of Ancient Nigeria.* New York: Alfred A. Knopf, 1980.

Exhibitions to be Held on the Occasion of the First International Congress of African Culture. Salisbury: National Gallery, 1962.

Fagg, Wiliam. *Nigerian Images.* New York: Frederick A. Praeger, 1963.

__________. *Yoruba Beadwork: Art of Nigeria.* New York: Rizzoli, 1980.

Fagg, William and John Pemberton III. *Yoruba Sculpture of West Africa.* ed. Bryce Holcombe. New York: Alfred A. Knopf, 1982.

Foss, Wilson Perkins. *The Arts of the Urhobo Peoples of Southern Nigeria.* Ann Arbor: University Microfilms, 1976.

Fraser, Douglas, ed. *African Art as Philosophy.* New York: Interbook, 1974.

Gillon, Werner. *Collecting African Art.* New York: Rizzoli, 1979.

Hersey, Irvin. *African Tribal Art from the Fred and Rita Richman Collection in the High Museum of Art.* Atlanta: The High Museum of Art, 1973.

Horton, Robin. *Kalabari Sculpture.* Lagos: Department of Antiquities, 1965.

__________. "The Kalabari Ekine Society: a Borderland of Religion and Art." *Africa.* 33(2): 94-114.

Houlberg, Marilyn H. "Ibeji Images of the Yoruba." *African Arts.* 7(1): 20-27, 91-92 (1973).

Lamp, Frederick. "African Art in the Baltimore Museum of Art." *African Arts.* 17(1): 32-46 (1983).

Lawal, Babatunde. *Yoruba Shango Sculpture in Historical Retrospect.* Ann Arbor: University Microfilms, 1971.

__________. "The Living Dead: Art and Immortality Among the Yoruba of Nigeria." *Africa.* 47(1): 50-61 (1977).

Leuzinger, Elsy. *Africa: The Art of Negro Peoples.* New York: Crown Publishers, 1967.

Lunsford, John. *The Gustave and Franyo Shindler Collection of African Sculpture.* Dallas: Dallas Museum of Fine Arts, 1975.

McCall, Daniel F. and Edna G. Bay, ed. *African Images: Essays in African Iconology.* New York: Africana, 1975.

McNaughton, Patrick. *Secret Sculptures of Komo: Art and Power in Bamana Initiation Associations.* Philadelphia: ISHI, 1979.

Meek, C. K. *A Sudanese Kingdom.* London: Kegan Paul, Trench, Trubner, and Co., 1931.

__________. *The Northern Tribes of Nigeria.* vol. I and II: New York. Negro Universities Press: 1925, rep. 1969.

Messenger, John C. "The Carver in Anang Society." in *The Traditional Artist in African Societies.* Warren d'Azevedo, ed. Bloomington: Indiana University Press, 1973, pp. 101-27.

Morton-Williams, Peter. "An Outline of the Cosmology and Cult Organization of Oyo Yoruba." *Africa.* 34: 243-61.

__________. "The Yoruba Ogboni Cult in Oyo." *Africa.* 30(4): 362-374 (1960).

Mount, Marshall. *African Art from New Jersey Collections.* Montclair: Montclair Art Museum, 1983.

Murdock, George Peter. *Africa: Its People and Their Culture History.* New York: McGraw-Hill, 1959.

Murray, K.C. "Ekpu: The Ancestor Figures of Oron, Southern Nigeria." *Burlington Magazine.* 89: 310-15 (1947).

Nadel, Sigfried. *Nupe Religions.* London: Routledge, Kegan Paul, Ltd., 1954.

Nyet, Francois. "Masques elephant et statuaire des Igbo." *Arts d'Afrique Noire.* 32: 29-45. (1978)

Nyet, Francois. *Masques 'Elephant' Igbo Nigeria.* Paris: Galerie Helene Kamer, 1980.

Ojo, G. J. Afolabi. "Traditional Yoruba Architecture." *African Arts.* 1(3): 14-17, 70-72 (1968).

__________. *Yoruba Culture.* Ibadan: University of Ife and University of London Press, 1966.

Ottenberg, Simon. *Masked Rituals of Afikpo.* Seattle: University of Washington Press, 1975.

Pemberton, John III. "A Cluster of Sacred Symbols: Orisa Worship Among the Igbomina Yoruba of Ila-Orangun." *History of Religions.* 17(1): 1-28 (1977).

Poynor, Robin. "Edo Influence on the Arts of Owo." *African Arts* 9(4): 40-45 (1976).

Prince, Raymond. "Curse, Invocation and Mental Health Among the Yoruba." *Canadian Psychiatric Association Journal.* 5(2): 65-79 (1960).

__________. "The Yoruba Image of the Witch." *Journal of Mental Science.* 107: 795-805 (1961).

Roche, L. E. "The de la Burde Collection." *African Arts.* 5(2): 66 (1972).

Roy, Christopher D. *African Sculpture-The Stanley Collection.* Iowa City: University of Iowa Museum of Art, 1979.

Rubin, Arnold. *African Accumulative Sculpture.* New York: Pace Gallery, 1974.

__________. *The Arts of the Jukun-Speaking Peoples of Northern Nigeria.* Ann Arbor: University Microfilms, 1970.

Salmons, Jill. "Mammy Wata." *African Arts.* 10(3): 8-15, 87-88 (1977).

Schadler, Karl-Ferdinand. *African Art.* Munich: Stadtsparkasse, 1976.

Scheinberg, Alfred. *Ekon Society Puppets: Sculptures for Social Criticism.* New York: Tribal Arts Gallery II, 1977.

__________. *Two Aspects of the Doubled Image in African Art.* New York: Tribal Arts Gallery II, 1976.

Schwartz, Nancy Beth A. *Mambilla-Art and Material Culture.* Milwaukee: Milwaukee Public Museum, 1972.

Seligman, Thomas K. and Kathleen Berrin. *The Bay Area Collects: Art from Africa, Oceania, and the Americas.* San Francisco: Fine Arts Museums of San Francisco, 1982.

Sieber, Roy. *Sculpture of Northern Nigeria.* New York: Museum of Primitive Art, 1961.

Sieber, Roy and Arnold Rubin. *Sculpture of Black Africa: The Paul Tishman Collection.* International Exhibitions Foundation, 1970.

Sieber, Roy and Tony Vevers. *Interaction: The Art Styles of the Benue River Valley and East Nigeria.* West Lafayette, IN: Gallery II, Purdue University, 1974.

Siroto, Leon. *African Spirit Images and Identities.* New York: Pace Primitive and Ancient Art, 1976.

Starkweather, Frank. *Traditional Igbo Art.* Ann Arbor: University of Michigan Press, 1966.

Stoll, Mareidi and Gert. *Ibeji: Twin Figures of the Yoruba.* Munich: Gert and Mareidi Stoll., 1980.

Thompson, Robert Farris. "Aesthetics in Traditional Africa." *Art News.* 66(9): 44-45, 63-67 (1968).

__________. *African Art in Motion.* Los Angeles: University of California, 1963.

__________. *Black Gods and Kings.* Bloomington: Indiana University Press, 1971, reprinted 1976.

__________. "The Sign of the Divine King." in *African Art and Leadership.* Douglas Fraser and Herbert Cole, eds. Madison: University of Wisconsin Press, 1972, pp. 227-60.

__________. "The Sign of the Divine King." *African Arts.* 3(3): 8-17, 74-80 (1970).

Ubah, C. N. "The Supreme Being, Divinities and Ancestors in Igbo Traditional Religion." *Africa.* 5(2): 90-105.

Uchendu, Victor. *The Igbo of Southeast Nigeria.* New York: Holt Rinehart and Winston, 1965.

Udo, Reuben K. *Geographical Regions of Nigeria.* Berkley: University of California Press, 1970.

Vogel, Susan. *Gods of Fortune, The Cult of the Hand in Nigeria.* New York: Museum of Primitive Art, 1974.

Vogel, Susan, ed. *For Spirits and Kings-African Art from the Paul and Ruth Tishman Collection.* New York: Metropolitan Museum of Art, 1981. (entries by Houlberg, Fagg, Walker, Wolff, Poyner, Peek, Niklin).

Wassing, Rene S. *The Arts of Africa.* London: Thames and Hudson, 1970.

Wescott, Joan. "The Sculpture and Myths of Eshu-Elegba." *Africa.* 32(4): 336-353.

Wittmer, Marcilene K. *Cameroon.* Charlotte: Mint Museum, 1977.

Wittmer, Marcilene K., and William Arnett. *Three Rivers of Nigeria.* Atlanta: High Museum of Art, 1978.

Photo credits: George Flemming: Cover, 24, 39, 41, 66, 89; Robin Poynor: A, C-H; Herbert Cole: B; Eliot Elisofon, National Museum of African Art, Eliot Elisofon Archives, Smithsonian Institution: I; Bob Hanson: 4-5, 27, 30, 50-51, 99; Fleur Hales Testa: 2, 16-17: Chicago Art Institute: 3, 85; Jerry L. Thompson, Metropolitan Museum of Art, New York: 6, 20, 58, 83: William Doyle Gallery: 8; David Allison: 9, 47; Pace Gallery: 10, 21, 26, 32, 38, 45, 70, 92; J. S. Hammer: 15; Thomas Feist: 29, 44, 59, 65, 68, 75, 86, 100; Carole A. Rosen, National Museum of African Art: 37; Gerald Jones: 46, 57, 61-64, 71, 95; Seattle Art Museum: 49, 81; Chris McNair: 52; Field Museum of Natural History: 53; Delmar Lipp: 54, 90; Richard Todd, UCLA Museum of Cultural History: 55; Al Mozell: 67, 77; Robert Young Studios, Indiana University Museum: 76; Charles Davis: 82, 87, 88; New Orleans Museum of Art: 91; Jerome Drown, High Museum of Art: 93.